Into the Abyss

LIFE AFTER THE BUBBLE

By

Graham Summers, MBA

ISBN: 979-8-9903775-0-9

For Lucia and Santi.

Contents

Introduction   vii

Part 1: The Everything Bubble Has Burst   1
Chapter 1: Covid-19 Forces Policymakers to Reveal
    Their Playbooks   3
Chapter 2: Lessons From Japan (Why the Fed Can
    NEVER Normalize)   37
Chapter 3: The Greatest Monetary Screw-up of All Time   65
Chapter 4: The Future of Monetary Policy   99

Part 2: How to Invest After the Bubble   137
Introduction   139
Chapter 5: Introduction to Stocks   157
Chapter 6: Strategies for Passive Investors   165
Chapter 7: On Active Stock Market Investing   177
Chapter 8: Strategies For Active Investors   187

Conclusion   211
Endnotes   213

Introduction

The #1 question (or complaint) I've received concerning my first book *The Everything Bubble: The Endgame for Central Bank Policy* has been *"that's great... but how do I invest based on this?"*

I didn't avoid that topic to be mischievous.

When I wrote *The Everything Bubble* in 2017, I didn't have an answer to that question. For one thing, it wasn't clear how the financial system would behave during the next crisis. Even more importantly, it wasn't clear how bold policymakers (the people in charge of introducing the regulations and monetary policies that affect the other 330 million of us) would be in terms of their policy response to said crisis.

Regarding how the financial system would respond to the next crisis:

- Would we experience another 2008-type deflationary event in which a major asset class (real estate, sovereign bonds, etc.) collapsed, dragging down the large financial firms and banks?

- Or would we finally see inflation arrive in the financial system, leading to a major sell-off in bonds as the Fed was forced to tighten monetary policy, thereby triggering a debt crisis?

- Or would China finally collapse due to all the shoddy debts in its shadow banking system, which in turn would trigger a run on the U.S. dollar and a deflationary spiral?

- Or would the automated trading strategies that have dominated the markets since 2008 be caught off-sides by a black swan event resulting in another severe crash similar to that of October 1987?

As different as the above crises sound, they all fall into one of two categories: an inflationary crisis or a deflationary crisis. The differences between those situations are dramatic as are the differences in the strategies an investor would need to employ to profit from them.

Think back to 2008.

At that time, the Fed cut interest rates to zero for the first time in history, while also launching its first-ever large-scale Quantitative Easing (QE) program to the tune of $1.25 trillion.

Based on this, many investors, including more than a few of the investing legends, believed that the ultimate outcome of the Fed's policy response would be inflation. After all, how could you make money so cheap, and print so much of it, without inducing an inflationary spike?

These inflationists were right… for a time. From 2009-2011, inflation expectations soared, driving many commodities, as well as precious metals like gold, to new all-time highs. Then Europe's banking system began to implode, the U.S. dollar caught a bid, and inflation was overwhelmed by a deflationary tidal wave.

It's worth noting that the Fed continued to keep rates at zero for another four years… while printing another $2 trillion… **but inflation still didn't show up, at least not in a systemic manner.**

Anyone who invested based on an inflationary framework during this time period was in a world of hurt. Peak to trough, from 2011 to their lows in 2020, gold and other inflation hedges lost some 70% of their value, while long-term U.S. treasury bonds, which should *collapse* during an inflationary episode, more than doubled in value!

In investing, one of the most important items, if not the most important item to understand is the framework in which the financial system is operating. As the above results illustrate, if you invest based on the wrong framework, you can lose a LOT of money for a VERY long period of time.

So again... the reason I didn't write about how to invest for when the Everything Bubble burst back in 2017 was simply because I didn't have an answer at the time. I'm a strategist, not a psychic. And while many in my profession try to act like they're the latter... the reality is that predictions aren't worth much if they don't actually result in investment profits.

Then the COVID-19 pandemic hit... and all of my questions about what future crises would look like, as well as how policymakers would respond to said crises, were answered.

The financial system's response to the pandemic and economic shutdowns was so rapid and so violent that policymakers were forced to show us their entire "playbook" in terms of how they really view the economy... as well as how far they were willing to go to stop a total meltdown.

The results were nothing short of staggering.

If you had told someone in 2017 that the U.S. would choose to *shut down its economy voluntarily*, inducing a severe recession *on purpose*, they likely would have told you to seek psychiatric help.

Similarly, if you had told that same person in 2017 that during the next crisis the Fed would not only buy U.S. Treasuries and Mortgage-Backed Securities as it did in 2008... but that it would also buy municipal bonds, corporate bonds, student loans, commercial paper, certificates of deposit, auto loans, and more... at a rate of $150 billion *per day*, they again would tell you to talk to a mental health professional.

All of those things happened. And what's really incredible is that practically everyone went along with it!

I suspect part of this was due to the speed at which everything unfolded. It's long been argued in policymaking circles that you can introduce truly extraordinary things provided the general public is adequately terrified.

The market meltdown triggered by the pandemic took this concept to the nth degree. Not only was the crisis severe (most of the economy was shut down) but it was also extremely rapid: whereas the 2008 Crisis took ~18 months to unfold, the pandemic-induced market crash took just SIX WEEKS.

Because of both the severity and the speed of this crisis, policymakers became so desperate that they implemented not just one or two, but practically ALL of the emergency policies they'd been dreaming of introducing to manage the economy/ financial system, **including the ones that were previously thought to be too politically toxic to be possible.**

In simple terms, the pandemic revealed how policymakers, *__really think about things.__*

We now know that policymakers believe:

1. That most of the economy can simply be turned off and on like a light-switch.

2. That Americans don't actually *need* to work, but that policymakers can "paper over" a depression with stimulus checks.

3. That small businesses (which every politician and policymaker claims to champion), are in fact nonessential and can be shut down without serious consequence.

4. That Fortune 500 businesses (which comprise the bulk of political donations), are considered "essential businesses" while small businesses are not.

And finally...

5. That the vast majority of Americans will tolerate all of the above policies being introduced without rioting, or kicking the political class who pushed this stuff on them out of office.

I want to be clear here. I am not saying that the above policies or views are morally right or even sane. I'm simply stating that the pandemic revealed how policymakers *really* think about things. And more importantly for us, we now know that policymakers are also willing to implement these policies if given the chance!

Indeed, as far as policymakers are concerned, the most important item in the above list is #5: the fact that no one got kicked out of office or was forced to resign for implementing these policies.

The first four items in the list (paying people to not work/using stimulus to finance consumer spending) had been written about in economics papers or discussed in central banking circles behind closed doors for decades... but policymakers had always been concerned that Americans wouldn't stand for them.

No longer.

As far as policymakers are concerned, the pandemic revealed that most Americans are far more willing to tolerate forced unemployment, economic central planning and a loss of individual freedoms than expected.

And while it's true that the COVID-19 pandemic was likely a "once in a lifetime" event, I expect that when the next financial crisis arrives, policymakers will push to implement similar policies to those they introduced in 2020, namely, picking and choosing which businesses are worthy of government support, doling out stimulus money and loans that don't need to be paid back to the tune of trillions of dollars, and pushing to silence or censor those who don't agree with these policies.

Yes, it's horrifying stuff, but at least we know the deal now. And as a strategist, I'd rather know what policymakers *really* think and what Americans are *really* willing to tolerate than try to guess either of those subjects. At the very least, this knowledge provides us with a framework for what's to come. And we can use that framework to implement investment strategies that will profit from these issues.

With that in mind, this book is a bit different from your typical book on central bank policy and investing.

The first four chapters are:

1. **COVID-19 Forces Policymakers to Reveal Their Playbooks:** We review the monetary and fiscal policies the U.S. central bank (the Federal Reserve or "the Fed") and federal government implemented during the pandemic.

2. **Lessons from Japan:** Japan is the grandfather of monetary policy insanity. Everything the Fed has done since 2008 was first tried by Japan a decade earlier. With that in mind, we review what Japan has already done because we know it's what the Fed will try to do when the next crisis hits.

3. **The Greatest Monetary Policy Screw-up of All Time:** When the Fed unleashed an inflationary storm from 2020 to 2022, it dramatically changed the investing landscape for years to come. We delve deep into what I consider to be the greatest monetary screw-up in 50 years as well as the implications of what it means for the financial system going forward.

4. **The Future of Monetary Policy:** I detail the monetary policies we can expect the Fed to introduce when things go south in the U.S. economy and financial markets in the future. Some of these policies represent a rebranding of prior extraordinary monetary measures. Others are completely new. But I expect all of them to be unveiled in the coming months and years.

You can think of these first four chapters as a kind of follow-up to my 2017 book, *The Everything Bubble: The Endgame for Central Bank Policy.*

As a quick aside, if you're new to finance, economics and investing, I strongly urge you to read that book before you read this one. The reason for this is that *The Everything Bubble* outlines many of the fundamental concepts pertaining to how our financial system operates. If you're unfamiliar with terms such as "the Fed" or "the Fed fund rate" or "Treasury yields" please read *The Everything Bubble* before proceeding with this book as I won't be reviewing those concepts here.

Don't be concerned, *The Everything Bubble* is not a dry or academic read. You'll likely rip through it in a day or two. You'll then be ready to read *Into The Abyss (Life After the Bubble)*.

The second portion of *Into The Abyss* will be devoted to helping you successfully navigate what's to come from an investing perspective. I'll be outlining the frameworks I use to help my clients navigate the Fed's cycles of bubbles and busts. I'll also be providing real-world tools and techniques you can use to improve your own investing whether you are a passive or active investor.

So, without further ado, let's put our fears aside, dive into the abyss that is the current worldview of fiscal and monetary policymakers, and map out how best to think and profit in life after the bubble.

PART 1:

The Everything Bubble Has Burst

CHAPTER 1

Covid-19 Forces Policymakers to Reveal Their Playbooks

IN MY 2017 bestselling book, *The Everything Bubble: The Endgame for Central Bank Policy*, I predicted that when the Everything Bubble burst, the Fed and other policymakers would go *nuclear* with monetary policy to reflate the bubble.

For those of you who are unfamiliar with my first book, a quick outline of its contents are as follows:

The current U.S. central bank, the Federal Reserve or "the Fed" for short, was created in 1913. Since that time, the U.S. financial system has been dominated by two primary themes:

1. The gradual shift from gold to U.S. government debt, called Treasuries, as the bedrock or senior-most asset class in the financial system.

2. The long-term devaluation of the U.S. dollar.

This system is great at some things, most notably generating cheap credit and "inflating debts away" by ensuring future dollars are worth less. However, it's terrible at other things such as growing incomes, creating jobs, generating economic growth, limiting obscene wealth inequality, etc.

From a systemic perspective, the biggest issue with this arrangement is that there is no defined limit to the amount of credit or debt that the U.S. can issue: once the U.S. completely severed ties between the U.S dollar and gold in 1971, all U.S. debt would be paid with paper money which the Fed could print at will.

Now, debt in of itself is not a problem, but excessive debt can be a *big* problem. And since the U.S. ended the Gold Standard in 1971, the growth in its debts has rapidly outpaced the growth of its economic activity as measured by Gross Domestic Product or GDP.

The below chart from *The Everything Bubble* demonstrates this well. By the time the mid-1990s rolled around, the U.S. financial system was completely saturated with debt.

Chart 1: US Gross Domestic Product vs. US Total Debt Securities, Trillion of US Dollars (1945-2016).

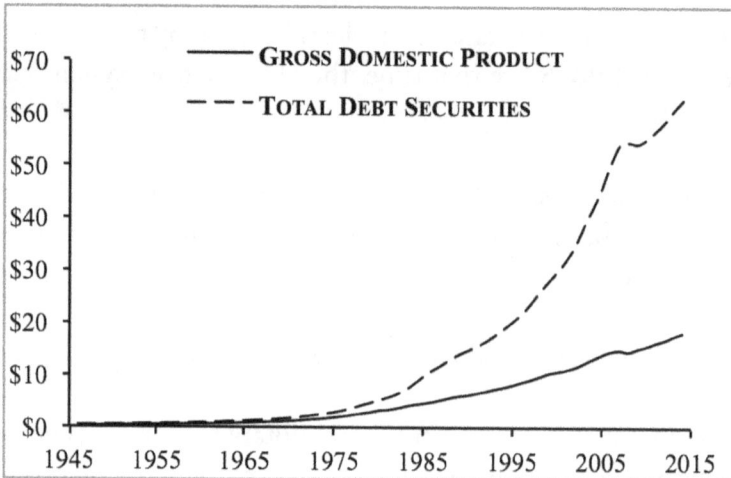

Note: Data adapted from the Federal Reserve Bank of St. Louis[1]

With so much debt in the system, any financial crisis had the potential to lead to a systemic event: a situation in which much, if not most, of the financial system would go into insolvency and fail. This is the dreaded "deflation" you sometimes hear about in the financial media. However, to be truly accurate, we're talking about debt deflation or the process through which debt becomes worth less, on its way to "worthless."

To give you an idea of how serious this issue can be, take note of the tiny dip in the dashed line in the chart above. That tiny dip represents the debt deflation of the Great Financial Crisis of 2008.

However, I'm getting ahead of myself here.

As I was saying, starting in the mid-1990s, the U.S. reached the point of debt saturation, or the point at which any financial crisis has the potential to trigger a systemic collapse. Because of this, the Fed has been forced to use ever-more aggressive monetary policies to stop financial crises from becoming systemic events.

This resulted in what I call the "Era of Serial Bubbles": a period in which the Fed allows/ creates a bubble in a major asset class, ignores the obvious signs that the bubble is a problem for far too long, and is then forced to create another, even larger bubble in an even more senior asset class when the first bubble bursts.

The most recent bubbles are:

1. The Technology Bubble of the 1990s: a bubble in U.S. stocks, particularly technology stocks related to the Internet. This bubble was obvious as early as 1996, but the Fed allowed it to continue for another four years until it finally burst, triggering a three-year bear market in stocks that erased trillions of dollars in wealth.

Of the last three major bubbles, this was the smallest as it was largely contained to the U.S. and its bursting did not become a global issue. However, the Tech Bubble was still a one in 100-year event in terms of stock market valuations and mania up until that point. And when it burst, the Fed created...

2. The Housing Bubble of the mid-2000s: a bubble in U.S. real estate, which represents the single largest financial transaction of most Americans' lives.

    This bubble, like the Tech Bubble before it, was obvious to practically everyone but the Fed, which stood idle while home prices hit levels that were three standard deviations away from their historic relationships to income.

    However, unlike the Tech Bubble, the Housing Bubble became a global issue due to the proliferation of "Over the Counter Derivatives" (OTC derivatives) through which Wall Street packaged up mortgages and sold them to other banks, financial institutions, hedge funds, etc., around the world. The OTC derivatives market for toxic mortgages was $50-$60 trillion at its peak and resulted in multiple large financial institutions requiring bailouts when it burst.

    When this bubble burst, the Fed created...

3. The bubble in U.S. Government Bonds, called Treasuries: a bubble in the senior-most asset class in our current financial system and by far the largest, most significant bubble of our lifetimes.

    Because the yields on these bonds represent the "risk-free" rate of return against which all risk assets are valued, when the Fed created a bubble in Treasuries, it was creating a bubble in

EVERYTHING. This is why I coined the term "the Everything Bubble" and made it the title of my first book.

This bubble, like the two before it, was obvious. And once again, the Fed opted to ignore it for far too long.

When I published *The Everything Bubble: The Endgame for Central Bank Policy* in 2017, I had thought the Everything Bubble would burst due to organic reasons, meaning the crisis would come from *within* the financial system.

This had been the case with both the Tech Bubble and Housing Bubble: in both instances the Fed *finally* acted to deflate the bubble (much too late, of course) by tightening monetary conditions at a very slow pace.

Despite the Fed's best efforts, both of these bubbles burst in spectacular fashion, resulting in investor panics that destroyed trillions of dollars' worth of wealth. Said crises only ended when the Fed enacted *extraordinary* monetary easing, resulting in the creation of another larger bubble in another more-senior asset class.

Again, this had been the case with both the Tech and the Housing Bubbles. So, I assumed it would be the case with the Everything Bubble. And from 2017-2019, it looked as if I was going to be right.

Running Down the "Bubble Checklist"

In 2017, the Fed had just completed nine years of the most extraordinary monetary policy in its history, keeping interest rates at zero (technically 0.0%-0.25%) for seven years (2008-2015) while simultaneously printing $3.5+ trillion in new money which it used to buy securities from Wall Street via a process called Quantitative Easing or QE.

At this point in time, things had reached the level of absurdity that is usually associated with bubbles.

The Fed had been telling Americans that the U.S. was in an economic recovery since the middle of 2009. However, throughout the time period in which the Fed was claiming this, it was *also* running emergency levels of monetary interventions. Most absurdly, in 2014 and 2015, a full six years into the "recovery," the Fed was running two open-ended QE programs worth $80 billion per month while also keeping interest rates near zero.

For those of you who don't think about central bank policy much (lucky you), allow me to explain just how absurd this situation was. At $80 billion per month, the QE programs the Fed was running as late as 2014 were the largest the Fed had performed in its ~100-year history. All told they amounted to nearly $1 TRILLION in money printing per year ($960 billion to be exact).

For the Fed to claim the economy was doing well while running this much QE is akin to a drug addict repeatedly stating, *"I'm fine, I definitely don't have a problem,"* while simultaneously pawning his family's furniture for cash to buy drugs.

Adding to the absurdity was the fact that the Fed had only raised rates once in 2015 and again in 2016 respectively, meaning that by 2017, nearly 10 years AFTER the Great Financial Crisis of 2008, **interest rates were still below 1%.**

Again, let me explain just how absurd this was.

Historically, the Fed usually CUTS interest rates down to 1% during major recessions or crises. The Fed did this during the 1958 recession, the 1967 recession and during the aftermath of the Tech Crash. The fact that the Fed had rates below 1% a full NINE years into what it claimed was an economic recovery, was **ludicrous**.

So, you can see just how absurd the Fed looked to any serious market participant or businessperson in 2017. For nearly a decade the Fed had been proclaiming that the economy was in recovery and that said recovery was strong... and yet the Fed was still printing ~$1 trillion per year while maintaining rates that were below levels usually associated with extraordinary monetary easing!

Worse still for the Fed, by this point everyone knew that its policies had created a massive bubble in Treasuries. It took the U.S. 232 years to rack up its first $10 trillion in debt. Thanks to the Fed's egregious monetary policies following the Great Financial Crisis, **the U.S. added another $10 trillion in debt in just nine years.**

Put simply, when I published *The Everything Bubble* in 2017, we had all the pieces in place for another deflationary bust like that of the Tech Crash of 2000 and the Great Financial Crisis of 2008. Those pieces were:

- The financial system was showing clear signs of a bubble? CHECK!

- The Fed was way behind the curve in terms of normalizing policy? CHECK!

- Everyone knew the Fed was way behind the curve to the point that the Fed was becoming something of a joke? CHECK!

- The Fed *finally* became aware of how far behind the curve it was and began rushing to normalize policy despite the fact the financial system had just experienced NINE YEARS of loose monetary conditions? CHECK!

Regarding that last point, between 2008 and 2017, the Fed raised rates by 0.25% a mere two times: once in 2015 and once again in 2016. Then sometime in early 2017, the Fed decided to get serious about normalizing things and raised rates by 0.25% three separate times that year. It then implemented another four rate hikes of 0.25% in 2018.

Simultaneously, the Fed began Quantitative Tightening (QT), a process through which it shrank its balance sheet by allowing the bonds it owned to mature. Upon maturation, the Fed would transfer the funds to the U.S. Treasury, thereby reducing liquidity in the financial system. By late 2018, the Fed had done this to the tune of ~$500 billion.

And that's when the stuff began to hit the fan.

In mid-2018, the bubble in Treasury bonds appeared to be bursting. At that point in time Treasury bonds fell to levels that suggested the 30+ year bull market in U.S. bonds was OVER… just as I had initially predicted.

The Everything Bubble was bursting, and the Great Treasury Crisis was about to begin!

Then the Fed completely reversed course and began *easing* monetary conditions before the real fireworks began. True, stocks dropped some 20% in the span of a few weeks at the end of 2018, **but the financial system never truly entered a full-scale crisis.**

Why?

The Fed "Pumps the Brakes" Before the Crisis Hits

We'll never know why the Fed shifted gears so quickly and began easing monetary policy in early 2019. It's possible the Fed was jumpy concerning a potential crisis due to the political fallout it had triggered with the bailouts it implemented following the 2008 Crisis.

Alternatively, the Fed may have acted quickly because the President of the United States in late 2018 was Donald Trump. And President Trump was **obsessed** with the stock market. He tweeted and talked about it on a near-daily basis. Heck, he even went so far as to harass Fed officials by name on Twitter (now X) because the Fed's rate hikes were resulting in his beloved stock market dropping!

Whatever the reason (perhaps the previously unscheduled dinner the Fed Chair and Vice-Chair had with President Trump in January 2019 was *persuasive*), Fed officials began a very public campaign of assuaging the markets, claiming that the Fed had tightened monetary policy enough, and that it would be ending the interest rate hikes and QT soon.

As if this wasn't astonishing enough, Fed officials also began talking about the Fed potentially *easing* monetary conditions just a few weeks later! To provide some perspective here, historically the Fed doesn't start talking about easing monetary conditions for months, if not a full year, after the completion of a rate-hike cycle.

In 2018, the Fed completed the rate-hike cycle by hiking rates for the last time on December 20th, 2018. Within **8 weeks**, every single Fed President who had been pushing for more rate hikes had dropped this language from his or her public statements. And other Fed officials were starting to talk about rate cuts or even introducing a new round of QE!

As a result of this, the Everything Bubble never fully burst, the U.S. financial system never entered a true crisis, and things chugged along as usual… and I was wrong, or much too early in my prediction of a major crisis (which, in the investment business, is the same thing as being wrong).

Indeed, by the look of things in mid-2019, the Fed was back in an easing cycle, cutting rates three times in the latter half of the year. Here again, the significance of this might be lost on those of you who don't focus on central bank policy for a living (again, lucky you).

When the Fed reversed course like this, it represented a major blow to its credibility. First and foremost, the Fed is the single largest employer of economics PhDs in the U.S. employing 400 economics PhDs who are supported by 150 research assistants. With this brain trust on payroll, the Fed, as an entity, is generally believed to know more about the economy than anyone. So, it doesn't inspire much confidence to see the Fed spend 18 months prattling on about how it's time to tighten monetary policy only to blow up the corporate bond market, crash stocks, and then frantically backpedal on all of its prior assertions.

This is akin to having a doctor with multiple degrees from Ivy League institutions advise you that you need to exercise, stop drinking alcohol, and eat a healthy diet for months… only to then call you one night at midnight and advise you to *stop* jogging and start a diet of fast food and liquor.

Suffice to say, you'd find yourself another doctor.

Secondly, the Fed is *supposed* to be politically independent. Regardless of whether President Trump's incessant complaining and tweeting had any real impact on Fed policy, **it certainly looked as if the Fed was bowing to his demands.**

Again, that's a tremendous blow to Fed credibility. You can't argue that you have a better grasp on the economy than anyone else, only to have the President, a man who *doesn't even have a PhD in economics*, prove to know more than you… or at the very least be the one calling the shots on economic policy. After all, if the President can simply dictate monetary policy, why even bother having a central bank?

Finally, the fact that the whole situation blew up in the Fed's face during the holidays was a public relations nightmare. No one wants to get a 20% discount on his or her 401(k) for Christmas. And certainly NO ONE wants to spend the holiday break watching the stock market.

So, I wasn't the only one who looked bad when the Fed reversed course and the Everything Bubble remained intact. The Fed, at best, looked as if it was controlled by President Trump and at worst, like a bunch of incompetents.

Then the truly unthinkable happened.

The financial system began to collapse, not because of a drop in Treasuries due to Fed tightening, but because an exogenous event (COVID-19) panicked policymakers into doing the truly unthinkable.

They shut down the economy *voluntarily*.

I warn you in advance, I'm getting out my soap box for the next section.

The Largest Economics Experiment in History to the Tune of Trillions of Dollars and Millions of Jobs

I'm on record as early as the spring of 2020 stating that the economic and monetary policy responses to covid will go down in history as one of the worst- if not THE worst- blunders in policymaking history.

I want to stress that I'm talking about *economic* issues here, not healthcare, or public health issues. I'm not a healthcare expert, so I cannot comment on whether the shutdowns were the right thing to do from a health perspective.

What I *do* know is that economies are not like light switches; you can't just turn them off and then on again without major consequences. And by "major consequences" I don't just mean a stock market crash (though that happened too); I mean long-term economic issues that result in mass human misery for years to come.

13

Put simply, when policymakers began shutting down the economy voluntarily, they were embarking on the largest economics experiment in history, to the tune of millions of jobs and trillions of dollars.

How so?

For one thing, in today's global economy, few if any companies manufacture the raw materials or individual components necessary for their finished goods. In laymen's terms, almost nobody makes something from "start to finish" anymore.

Instead, companies rely extensively on other companies which are often located in different states, if not different countries, for their supplies.

A few well-known examples of this include:

a. BMW has over 12,000 suppliers located in 70 countries.

b. Apple has over 200 suppliers located everywhere from Tennessee to Brussels to China.

c. Proctor & Gamble has a jaw-dropping 50,000 suppliers around the world.

When policymakers chose to shut down the economy, they were rolling the dice that somehow all these different suppliers, located in different places, the economies of which would reopen on different schedules, **would somehow be able to continue producing things without a hitch.**

Now, you could argue that policymakers were not concerned with this kind of issue. After all, if COVID-19 was a naturally occurring, extremely deadly virus, or worse still, a bioweapon *designed to kill people*, then the supply chain would be the last thing on your mind.

My answer to that argument is that policymakers allowed many large businesses to remain in operation. Indeed, the defining rule for the lockdowns appears to have been that big businesses (the Amazons, Walmarts, and Apples of the world) could remain open, while Mom and Pop small businesses were all forced to close. The fact that the businesses that were permitted to remain open account for tens of millions in lobbying dollars to policymakers is just coincidence, I'm sure.

I realize I sound quite cynical here, so let's be a big more diplomatic. Assuming there was a chance that the covid virus was a bioweapon that accidentally leaked from a lab, <u>then yes, policymakers were 100% justified in closing the economy at first.</u>

However, as early as June of 2020 and most certainly by August of 2020, there were **clear signs** that the benefits of shutting down the economy ("stopping the spread, flattening the curve, etc.") were minimal. Meanwhile the costs were gargantuan in terms of suicides, overdoses, depression, divorces, etc., not to mention the psychological damage and developmental delays inflicted upon children. Indeed, the policy response to covid might very well be the first time in modern history that a "civilized" society put the needs of the elderly and adults before those of children.

Simply put, as early as the summer of 2020 and most certainly by early autumn 2020, the decision to keep the economy closed was not only foolish, but inhumane. And breaking the supply chain was not the only consequence of doing this; <u>policymakers were also smashing the labor market with a wrecking ball.</u>

I wrote earlier that economies are not light switches; you can't just flip them off and then back on again without causing major damage. The reason for this is because economies **are not machines**. In fact, economies are not "things" at all: an economy is simply a concept used to describe *human* activity concerning how we spend our time (making things or providing services) and our money (buying goods and services from others).

So, if you're going to shut down the economy, tell people to stay home, pay them not to work, and scare them out of their minds 24/7 with stories of dead bodies piling up and hospitals being overrun, **you're going to dramatically change how people choose to spend their time and their money.**

For one thing, if people are terrified and fear for their lives, they're going to start doing some soul-searching regarding how they are spending their lives. Many of them will decide that they don't particularly like their jobs and will either A) find new careers or B) not go back to work at all.

This played out as you would expect… particularly in sectors of the economy that aren't high paying and couldn't transfer to "work from home," e.g. unloading cargo ships, mining for coal, driving trucks, etc.

For instance, at one point in mid-2021, more than 70 cargo ships were stuck waiting to dock in L.A. while dozens more were stuck offshore of New York. The reason for this was that dock workers were among the groups of people who were paid more *not* to work via stimulus programs or who simply decided they'd rather move on to other work rather than go back to unloading cargo ships.

Sadly, docks were not the only segment of the economy suffering from labor issues. Even when cargo ships were being unloaded, there was a shortage of trucks available to transport goods to their final destinations. Truckers were also among the people choosing to change careers, or to not go back to work at all.

But wait… we're just getting started here.

In mid-2021, a full year into the lockdowns there were 8.6% fewer coal miners working than there were before the pandemic. You might not think this matters, but it does: coal accounts for ~20% of electricity generation in the U.S.

Natural gas accounts for another 40% of electricity generation... and the Oil and Gas industry was also struggling to get people to return to work. In 2020 some 115,000 oil and gas employees were laid off. By late 2021, only about a third of them had returned to work.

And remember, oil isn't just used to drive cars or power airplanes. Oil and oil derivatives are present in lipstick, Vaseline, solar panels, polyester (stain-resistant clothes), chewing gum, crayons, Aspirin, pantyhose, sneakers, detergent, CDs, concrete/cement, plastics of any kind, food additives, fertilizers, pesticides, candles, milk cartons, pen ink, and more.

I could go on and on here, but you get the point. Practically every industry has struggled and continues to struggle to find quality employees. As late as August 2023, over two years into the pandemic and four months AFTER the Biden administration declared that covid was no longer an emergency, the U.S. economy had 9.6 million job openings and only 6.4 million unemployed people. Historically, prior to covid, there were usually more unemployed people than job openings.

How is this possible?

Because people decided to find new jobs, stop working altogether for a time, or go into day-trading or some other stay-at-home venture. After all, if you're going to pay people NOT to work for the better part of two years, you cannot act surprised when those same people stop looking for jobs or move on to completely different career paths.

Again, when policymakers shut down the economy to "flatten the curve" for covid, they were embarking on the single largest economics experiment in history (inducing unfathomable human misery, psychological trauma, substance/alcohol abuse and more).

The fact that policymakers didn't anticipate this situation when they pushed to shut down the economy and keep it shut down for roughly two years says a lot about their understanding of economics and people.

Unfortunately, shutting down the economy didn't just mess up supply chains and the labor markets, **it also burst the Everything Bubble.**

It Truly Is Different This Time

There's an adage in investing that anytime someone says, *"you don't understand, it's different this time,"* you should sell everything.

The idea behind this is that any time investors start to abandon common sense or discard frameworks that have worked for decades, it's usually a sign that the market is in a kind of mania and a crisis is coming.

Well, it truly was *different this time* when policymakers decided to shut down the economy *voluntarily*. The U.S. economy wasn't shut down in the Revolutionary war, the Civil War, World War 1, World War 2, or any other major armed conflict.

Similarly, the U.S. economy wasn't shut down during the Cholera epidemics of 1832-1866 (which killed 5%-10% of people in large cities)[1], nor the Spanish flu of 1918 (which killed double the percentage of population allegedly killed by covid), nor any of the other pandemics.

---

1   https://www.healthline.com/health/worst-disease-outbreaks-history#cholera

Historical comparisons aside, when the U.S. shut down its economy in response to covid, it had two primary effects:

1. It turned one problem (a pandemic) into several (a pandemic, economic recession, stock market crash, etc.).

2. It forced policymakers to reveal their entire "playbook," rather than just a page or two of how to deal with crises.

Regarding #1, to be fair, a pandemic, even without shutdowns would result in a weaker economy (people would be terrified), significant stock market drop (ditto), and more. However, the decision to shut down the economy made these issues unfold more rapidly and in a more violent fashion.

Let's focus on the financial system and monetary policy here.

From an asset price perspective, the prior two bubbles (the Tech Bubble of the late '90s and the Housing Bubble of the '00s) burst over the span of **several years**.

In the case of the Tech Crash, technology stocks peaked in March of 2000. However, they didn't go straight down: there were massive draw-downs and face-ripping rallies for months on end, with the final bottom hitting two and a half years later. By that time, the NASDAQ had lost nearly 80% of its value.

Similarly, when the Housing Bubble burst, things took years to come to a head.

Housing prices peaked in July 2006. Roughly 12 months later, the first signs of major trouble in the subprime mortgage market surfaced when two Bear Stearns hedge funds went bust. Eight months later, Bear Stearns itself had to be absorbed by J.P. Morgan via a shotgun wedding in a single weekend. And six months after that, the mortgage giants Fannie Mae and Freddie Mac were placed into conservatorship while Lehman Brothers and AIG went bust. At that point the entire financial system began to implode.

Add it all up and both the Tech Bubble and the Housing Bubble took over two years to burst. By way of contrast, thanks to the economic shutdowns in 2020, **the Everything Bubble burst in the span of two to three weeks.**

Again, it *was* different this time. And not just in terms of speed. As I outlined in #2 in the list above, the fallout from the shutdowns was so dramatic, that it forced policymakers to reveal their entire "playbook."

Let me explain…

A Brief History of Monetary Insanity

When the Tech Crash hit in 2000, the Fed dealt with the issue by gradually cutting interest rates down to 1%. At that point in history, the Fed had yet to attempt a large-scale Quantitative Easing (QE) program. Indeed, had someone suggested the Fed do one at the time, he or she would have likely been labelled a lunatic.

Fast forward eight years to the Great Financial Crisis of 2008, and the Fed cut interest rates below 1% to zero (0.0%-0.25%). This was the famed Zero Interest Rate Policy (ZIRP) policymakers had dreamed of implementing in the U.S. for years. This development was a major landmark in terms of how extreme the Fed was willing to go to stop a crisis from triggering a systemic event.

In 2008, the Fed also introduced a large-scale QE program… and I do mean LARGE: the first program, announced in November 2008, eventually grew to $1.25 trillion or roughly the size of Canada's GDP at the time.

QE involved the Fed using newly printed money to buy Mortgage-Backed Securities (MBS), agency debt (debt from the mortgage giants Fannie Mae and Freddie Mac) and U.S. Treasuries from financial institutions. The Fed would subsequently spend another $2+ trillion buying MBS and Treasuries over the next nine years. At that point in time, this was the most extreme monetary policy in the Fed's history.

Then came the shutdowns.

The Fed's policy response to the pandemic was so extreme, it was technically *illegal*. I'm not exaggerating here, **by law** the Fed is not permitted to buy any assets aside from Treasuries and *maybe* Mortgage-Backed Securities.

During the market meltdown triggered by the shutdowns, the Fed announced it would be buying both of those securities as well as municipal debt, corporate debt, student loans, auto loans, certificates of deposit, commercial paper and more. Indeed, as a friend of mine joked at the time, **the only asset class the Fed *wasn't* buying was old NFL contracts.**

And it all took place in the span of a single month. Not two years as was the case with the Tech Crash and Housing Crash, but **a single month.** Again, it truly *was different* this time.

During a typical crisis, the Fed would reveal just a page or two from its playbook for dealing with financial crises (ZIRP, QE, etc.). However, the shutdowns and the subsequent economic/ financial fallout happened so rapidly that the Fed was forced to reveal its **entire playbook**.

And *that* is something we can use to frame our thinking and our investments going forward!

However, given the speed of this situation as well as the extreme nature of what the Fed did in March-April of 2020, it's extremely likely most Americans didn't even catch it. After all, who wants to pay attention to whether the Fed is violating the Federal Reserve Act of 1913 when there's a pandemic underway, everyone is terrified of dying, and the financial system is imploding?

So, to fully digest what happened, let's do a quick review of the crisis and how the Fed responded to it.

The Shutdowns Burst the Everything Bubble

Prior to the economic shutdowns, the U.S. economy was chugging along quite well.

In January 2020, the unemployment rate had just hit an all-time low of 3.5%, while GDP growth was decent at 2+%, and the stock market was at an all-time high.

The pandemic and subsequent economic shutdowns erased these positive developments in the span of a few weeks. And I do mean *weeks:* within six weeks of policymakers implementing shutdowns, over 20 million Americans were unemployed, GDP had crashed by an astonishing 33%, and the financial system was experiencing its first bout of systemic risk since the depths of the Great Financial Crisis of 2008.

Now, as I mentioned a few pages ago, the phrase "the Everything Bubble" refers to a bubble in U.S. government bonds, which are also called Treasuries.

By quick way of review, these bonds serve as the bedrock of the current financial system; their yields represent the "risk-free" rate of return against which all risk assets (stocks, corporate bonds, municipal bonds, real estate, etc.) are priced.

So, when the Fed created a bubble in Treasuries following the Great Financial Crisis of 2008, it was *technically* creating a bubble in every risk asset... hence why I coined the term "the Everything Bubble."

Think of it this way, if Treasury yields are extraordinarily low because of Fed policy, every risk asset that trades based on this false level of risk is going to be mispriced. So, technically speaking, the Everything Bubble was in fact a kind of mega bubble comprised of lots of smaller, secondary bubbles in numerous risk assets such as corporate bonds, municipal bonds, and the like.

In 2020, when policymakers opted to shut-down the economy to "flatten the curve" for covid, many of these secondary bubbles began to burst.

Within a few weeks, the financial system was experiencing a crisis in...

1. The high-yield corporate debt markets: these are bonds that are issued by corporations with low credit ratings. Some of the more famous companies with junk debt ratings are Ford and Netflix.

2. The investment-grade corporate debt markets: these are bonds that are issued by high quality corporations with strong credit ratings. Think Microsoft or Apple.

3. The high-yield municipal bonds markets: these are bonds that are issued by municipalities (cities, towns, states) with low credit ratings. Think Chicago.

4. The investment-grade municipal bond markets: these are bonds that are issued by wealthy municipalities (cities, towns, states)

with high credit ratings. San Antonio is a well-known city with this debt rating.

I realize some of the above terms are rather esoteric... so, think of the situation this way: when policymakers shut down the economy, multiple trillion-dollar (with a "t") debt bubbles began bursting all at once.

The debt markets weren't the only ones under duress either: stocks experienced their most rapid 30% decline in history. Neither the Crash of 1929, nor Black Monday of 1987 saw stocks lose so much value so quickly.

It truly was a market meltdown.

While stocks got most of the attention because over 50% of Americans' retirement accounts are invested in that asset class, the reality is that in the larger, more systemically important debt markets we just outlined, the financial system was rapidly approaching a "systemic event" or total collapse.

Let me provide some perspective on the term "systemic".

The Shutdowns Also Triggered Systemic Risk

While stocks might be the most popular asset class for investors, they are actually one of the smallest asset classes in the financial system. Depending on stock price levels, the total value of the U.S. stock market ranges from $20-$50 trillion in size.

Now, at the time of the COVID-19 pandemic, U.S. stocks were worth about $35 trillion. Meanwhile, the total amount of debt securities in the U.S. was worth more than twice this amount ($77 trillion).

And during the 2020 meltdown, more than $13 trillion of this was imploding: $10 trillion in corporate bonds, $3.8 trillion in municipal bonds and another $1.2 trillion in senior secured loans.

Bear in mind, I'm not even bothering to include mortgages, credit cards, student loans, auto loans, and other lesser debt markets that were also collapsing due to the economic fallout from the pandemic. If we were to include those debt instruments as well, the true value of "at risk" assets would be much greater than $13 trillion.

Now, in today's world of massive Fed interventions and fiscal insanity, the word "trillion" doesn't hold the same weight as it used to. So, to put this $13 trillion figure into perspective, the U.S. economy was about $22 trillion in size in 2020, so we're talking about an amount of debt equal to roughly 60% of the country's total annual economic output entering a free fall, not over the course of a year, **but over the course of a few days.**

And the systemic risk didn't stop there.

I mentioned Over The Counter (OTC) derivatives earlier in this book (these are the securities that nearly blew up the financial system in 2008). Well, Wall Street and other large financial institutions never stopped creating or trading those things. And in 2020, when the debt markets began to implode **there were over $146 TRILLION worth of derivatives trading based on bond yields in the U.S. alone.**

Now, *that* number is truly incomprehensible. So, to provide some context here, consider that the OTC derivatives market that caused the Great Financial Crisis of 2008 was $50-$60 trillion in size.

Suffice to say, the 2020 market meltdown had the potential to be exponentially worse than the Great Financial Crisis of 2008. We are talking about truly *systemic* risk, as in the entire financial system collapsing.

Obviously, the Fed had to act fast to contain this situation. However, no one, not even the most crazed conspiracy theorist, could have predicted what the Fed would do.

Unlimited QE: Monetary Policy so Outlandish It Was *Technically* Illegal

One of the most important things to know about the stock market is that it is forward-looking, meaning it discounts the future.

In late February 2020, the stock market was discounting a future of shutdowns and economic depression. The first state to issue a "stay home" order was California on March 19th. However, stocks had already lost 30% by the time this order was issued!

And as I mentioned a few pages ago, stocks weren't the only asset class collapsing at this time. Corporate bonds, municipal bonds, oil, gold, practically anything you can name was in a free-fall.

To combat this crisis, on March 3rd, the Fed announced an emergency rate cut of 0.5%.

When that proved to be inadequate, the Fed announced a second, even larger rate cut of 1.0%, bringing interest rates back to zero (0.00%-0.25%) on March 15th. That same day, the Fed announced a $700 billion QE program.

The Fed also opened several credit facilities to provide liquidity to the commercial paper and money market industries (both of these industries are involved in the trading of very short-term debt securities).

When that didn't stop the bloodbath, the Fed announced it would buy everything.

And I do mean EVERYTHING.

On Monday March 23rd, 2020, the Fed staged an Emergency Meeting during which it announced that it would be expanding its $700 billion QE program to "unlimited" … **meaning it would print as much money and buy as many assets as needed.**

The Fed announced it would use this unlimited QE to fund credit facilities that would buy:

- Mortgage-Backed Securities (MBS)
- U.S. Treasuries
- Corporate debt (debt issued by corporations)
- Corporate debt-related ETFs (stock funds linked to corporate debt)
- Municipal debt (debt issued by states, counties, and cities)
- Certificates of Deposit (CDs)
- Student Loans
- Auto Loans
- More…

The Fed also announced it would soon be introducing a bailout program for small- and medium-sized businesses. And as if that wasn't enough, the Fed stated that it was lowering the interest rate it charged on its repo programs (vehicles through which the Fed allows financial institutions to park assets with the Fed in exchange for cash) to actually ZERO.

It's difficult to put into words just how extraordinary all of this is. So, let me provide a little perspective.

The Fed was created in 1913. Prior to the economic shutdowns of 2020, the greatest financial crisis the Fed had faced during its ~100-year history was that of the Great Financial Crisis of 2008.

As I noted earlier in this chapter, to combat that situation, the Fed introduced Zero Interest Rate Policy (ZIRP) and printed some $3.5 trillion over the course of seven years. The Fed used this money to buy Mortgage-Backed Securities (MBS) and Treasuries from financial firms via Quantitative Easing (QE) programs.

During the very depths of the 2008 crisis, the Fed also backstopped liabilities and bought stock in several large banks (Bank of America, Citigroup, etc.) while intervening directly in the money market fund and commercial paper markets.

So... all in all, the tab for "fixing" the Great Financial Crisis was seven years of ZIRP and $3.5 trillion in QE with a few emergency lending facilities opened to prop up the large Wall Street banks. This no longer sounds obscene, but at the time, this was truly extraordinary monetary policy... something that few if any people believed was possible.

Fast forward to 2020 and the Fed was back to buying both Treasuries and MBS as well as:

1. Corporate debt from individual companies like Apple, Toyota, etc.

2. Corporate debt that was packaged into Exchange Traded Funds (ETFs) which trade in the stock markets.

3. Municipal debt issued by cities, states, and municipalities.

4. Bundles of Certificates of Deposit (CDs).

5. Bundles of Student Loans.

6. Bundles of Auto Loans.

7. Money market funds.

8. Commercial paper.

And more!

How did it do this? After all, the Federal Reserve Act of 1913 *explicitly* forbids the Fed from buying these assets.

The Fed got around this issue by working with the U.S. Treasury through various credit facilities. The details of these facilities are quite technical, so for our purposes think of them as working like this: the Fed printed money, gave the money to the Treasury, and the Treasury then bought the assets.

Astonishing. But the *pace* of the Fed's money printing was even more astonishing.

Welcome to NUCLEAR QE: the Fed Prints $3 Trillion in Just Three Months

As I mentioned earlier in the chapter, during the Great Financial Crisis of 2008, the single largest monetary intervention the Fed implemented was QE 1, through which it printed $1.25 trillion and used it to buy Mortgage-Backed Securities (MBS), Agency debt (debt from the mortgage giants Fannie Mae and Freddie Mac), and U.S. Treasuries.

The Fed followed this up with three other monetary programs called QE 2, Operation Twist, and QE 3, which spent another $2.25 trillion between 2009 and 2014, **bringing the Fed's total money printing to $3.5 trillion in seven years.**

During the pandemic, the Fed printed ~$3 trillion in just a little over THREE MONTHS.

But wait, it gets even more insane.

At the peak of its money printing following the Great Financial Crisis of 2008, the Fed was printing $80 billion per month. In contrast, at one point during the pandemic, the **Fed was printing $150 billion PER DAY.** And when it was all said and done, the Fed would print nearly $5 TRILLION in about 20 months.

I realize that this is difficult to imagine. After all, we're talking about trillions, or thousands of billions of dollars here. So let me provide you with a visual to help picture this insanity.

Below is a chart showing the growth of the Fed's balance sheet over the last 15 years. As I mentioned before, when the Fed engages in QE, it prints new money and uses it to buy assets. As a result of this, the Fed's balance sheet grows. Thus, the Fed balance sheet serves as a decent proxy for how much money the Fed is printing or has printed in the past.

Chart 2: Total Assets of Federal Reserve Banks, Trillions US Dollars (2006-2022)

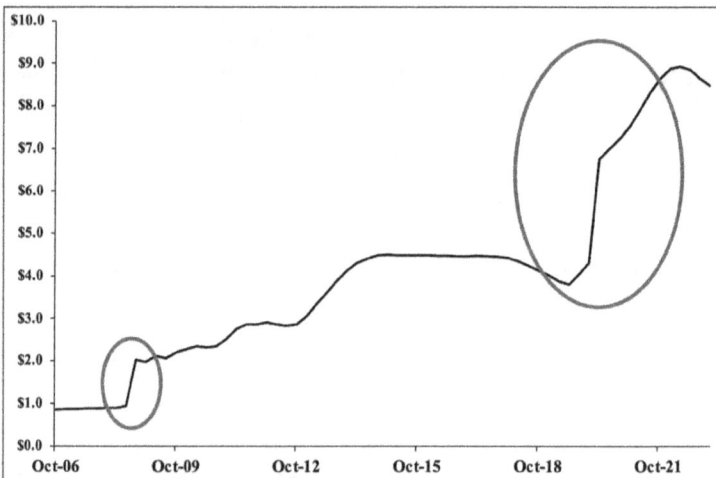

Note: Data adapted from the Federal Reserve Bank of St. Louis[2]

The small circle on the left side of the chart represents how much "money" the Fed printed during the 2008 market meltdown. Now, compare that to the oval on the right side of the chart, which represents how much "money" the Fed printed during the first seven months of the pandemic.

Again, this was truly jaw-dropping stuff. If you'd predicted any of this prior to 2020, most people (central bankers included) would have said that you were insane. However, as disturbing as the Fed's actions were, they did provide us with one benefit…

They gave us the entire playbook for how policymakers will respond to every crisis going forward.

Covid Gives Us the Fed's ENTIRE "Crisis Playbook"

Central bankers are a crafty bunch.

In public they try to appear calm, collected, and on top of things. But the reality is that "behind the scenes" they spend a lot of their time overseeing armies of economics PhDs who produce all kinds of research suggesting all kinds of crazy policies.

For instance, did you know that the Fed has been talking about banning cash as far back as 2001? Or that the Fed has known for over 20 years that the official inflation measure, the Consumer Price Index or CPI, is terrible at predicting future inflation? Or that the Fed believes it should use monetary policy to fight climate change?

You get the idea.

Unless you spend your days sifting through this stuff, you'd never know the Fed was up to any of this. The only way you'd find out would be when a crisis hit, and the Fed used the situation to introduce some crazy policy that it had been developing for years. And by then, you'd be so concerned about the markets wiping out your 401(k), you probably wouldn't even question the Fed's decision to implement this stuff!

As I mentioned in the introduction to this book, the primary reason why I didn't include investment ideas in my first book was because it wasn't clear what the Fed would do during the next financial crisis.

I had, at best, only one or two pages of the Fed's "crisis playbook" to work with (rate cuts and QE). Sure, I knew about the crazy policies the Fed was researching (negative interest rates, cash bans, etc.), but it wasn't clear the Fed would have the political capital to put those plans into motion.

No longer.

Because the crisis induced by the shutdowns was so rapid, it forced the Fed to reveal its entire playbook. I can now confidently say that the Fed has given us a clear path to follow in terms of how it will deal with any future financial crises.

The Fed's path?

Print enormous amounts of money and use it to buy **any** asset class that begins to collapse regardless of the legality of its actions.

Or… to put it even more simply: <u>print money.</u>

Indeed, once you start looking at how the shutdowns and subsequent economic fallout unfolded, it's clear that printing money is pretty much the only policy that Fed officials can come up with for solving economic woes.

Corporate bonds are collapsing, resulting in a potential crisis in the $10 trillion corporate bond market?

Fed response: Print money and use it to buy those bonds.

Municipal bonds are breaking down because the U.S. economy is weakening, and tax revenues won't be adequate to pay back city or county bondholders?

Fed response: Print money and use it to buy those bonds.

Asset-backed securities consisting of bundles of student loans or auto loans are being dumped because the banks don't believe Americans will be able to finance those loans due to an economic depression?

Fed response: Print money and use it to buy those assets.

It might sound as if I'm being facetious here until you consider that if you add up all of the money the U.S. has ever printed in its history… **over 40% of it was printed in 2020.**

And as if that isn't incredible enough, the Fed continued to engage in this monetary insanity for another ~20 months *AFTER* the economy began to recover!

According to the U.S. Bureau of Economic Analysis (BEA), the recession induced by the shutdowns ended in the second quarter of 2020. Despite this, the Fed continued to engage in a $120 billion monthly QE program up until November of 2021.

Yes, $120 BILLION per month, or roughly **$4 billion per day,** which was 50% larger than the largest QE program the Fed ran following the Great Financial Crisis ($80 billion per month). And the Fed continued to do this despite the economy being over a year into recovery and multiple asset classes (home prices, stocks, etc.) hitting new all-time highs! In fact, the Fed didn't actually stop printing money (albeit at a slower pace) until March of 2022!

The Fed was not the only entity engaged in nuclear levels of intervention. You've probably noticed that throughout this chapter I refer to "policy-makers" not "central bankers." There's a reason for this.

Uncle Sam Makes the Fed Look Like a Bunch of Money Printing Amateurs

As much as I like to rip on the Fed, the fact is that its policy response to the pandemic was relatively tame compared to what the Federal Government did.

Under the Trump administration, the Federal Government issued a $2.2 trillion stimulus package, the CARES Act in March 2020. This was the largest stimulus package in U.S. history. Indeed, it was so massive that in three months in 2020, the U.S. increased its deficit by more than it had during the **previous five recessions combined**.

The Trump administration followed this up with a *second* stimulus package, the CARES Act 2, worth $900 billion in December 2020. Up until this point the Federal Government was engaged in roughly the same amount of money printing ($3 trillion) as the Fed.

But Uncle Sam wasn't done yet.

The Biden administration introduced yet *another* stimulus package, The American Rescue Plan Act of 2021, worth $1.9 trillion in March 2021. Eight months later, President Biden would sign a $1.2 trillion infrastructure program into law. And less than a year after that came the ironically named *Inflation Reduction Act* which would spend another ~$400 billion.

Throw in the Fed's ~$5 trillion in money printing and you're talking about a combined **~$11 TRILLION in QE/stimulus being spent in the**

span of 20 months. This is a staggering amount of money equal to over 52% of the U.S.'s GDP in 2020.

There is no way the U.S. can return from this.

I'm not saying that to be gloom and doom, as in the U.S. is "finished" or "doomed." What I am saying is that the U.S. has entered a new era or "normal" as far as monetary policy is concerned. What was previously unthinkable e.g. "unlimited QE, the Fed buying assets outside the scope of its legal mandates, etc." has now been normalized. And there is little if any chance that the Fed will ever be able to return to what was considered "normal" prior to this.

To fully understand what I mean by that, we must turn our attention to the grandfather of monetary insanity, Japan.

CHAPTER 2

Lessons From Japan (Why the Fed Can NEVER Normalize)

JAPAN IS THE grandfather of monetary policy insanity.

Everything that the Fed and other western central banks implemented in response to the Great Financial Crisis of 2008 (ZIRP and QE), Japan's central bank had already been doing for 10-15 years.

The reason for this is that Japan experienced the first modern credit bubble in the 1980s, decades before anyone else. In a single decade, Japan experienced the equivalent of the U.S.' Tech Bubble of the 1990s and the U.S.' Real Estate Bubble of the '00s simultaneously.

Why did things get so out of control in Japan during this decade?

Four words: the Bank of Japan.

The Bank of Japan, or BoJ for short, is Japan's central bank. It was founded in 1882 and spent its first 100 years introducing, then abandoning, and then re-introducing the Gold Standard. Throughout this time Japan experienced booms and busts just like every other country. But it wasn't until the 1980s that things began to *really* go off the rails.

In truth, we could devote an entire multi-volume set of books to what happened in Japan in the 1980s. For the sake of time and space, the simplest rendering of the situation is as follows:

Japan dramatically cut regulations to open its economy and markets to foreign capital. Japanese banks lowered lending standards to the point of issuing credit to entities and people who had little if any chance of ever paying the loans back. And the BoJ fueled the entire thing by maintaining easy monetary policies for years despite the obvious signs that things were getting out of control.

How out of control?

At one point the land under the Emperor's Palace (roughly 1.3 square miles) **was "worth" more than the real estate in the entire State of California.** Moreover, despite being 1/26th the size of the U.S., Japan's real estate market was worth over FOUR times that of the U.S.

Real estate wasn't the only segment of Japan's economy that was egregious in its frothiness. Japan's stock market, called the Nikkei, rose almost 500% during that decade. We're not talking about an individual company… **we're talking about the ENTIRE stock market rising at a pace of more than 25% per year for an entire decade.**

By the time 1989 rolled around, eight of the 10 largest companies in the world were Japanese, and Japan accounted for nearly HALF (45%) of the global stock market by value, despite its economy only representing about 10% of global GDP ($3.05 trillion out of ~$37 trillion).

But wait, it gets even crazier…

In 1989, the seven largest banks in the world were Japanese. Nearly two thirds (16 out of 25) of the largest banks in the world were headquartered in Japan. And Japanese banks accounted for 40% of GLOBAL banking assets.

Again, we're talking about an economy that accounts for just 10% of global GDP, **with a banking system that accounts for 40% of global banking assets.** This bubble was truly staggering in its size and obvious to anyone paying attention as early as 1987. And yet, the BoJ didn't do a thing to stop this for another two years.

Once the BoJ finally *did* decide to try and calm things down, it didn't just ease into things. Instead, it moved aggressively, **raising interest rates from a low of 2.5% to 6% within just 18 months.**

What followed is precisely what you would expect: the bubbles in Japanese stocks and Japanese real estate burst in spectacular fashion.

Japan's stock market, the Nikkei, peaked in December of 1989. In less than a year (nine months to be precise) it had lost 46% of its value. Remember, we're not talking about a speculative tech start-up here... we're talking about the ENTIRE Japanese stock market losing nearly half its value in nine months.

Japanese real estate peaked a little over a year later in 1991. The collapse here was more of a "death of a thousand cuts" process as opposed to a crash (though certain metropolitan areas in Japan did experience crashes in real estate values). Japan property values would spend the next **20 years** in a downward trend... not finding a bottom until the 2010s.

As these bubbles imploded, the BoJ had a choice:

1. Let the financial system collapse, clear the bad debts, and then start over,

or...

2. Prop up Japan's markets and debt-ridden businesses with ultra-low interest rates (ZIRP) and Quantitative Easing (QE).

The BoJ chose #2.

The BoJ Boldly Goes Where No Central Bank Has Gone Before

As the Nikkei, Japanese real estate markets, and Japanese economy de-flated in the early '90s, the BoJ embarked on a campaign that would later be copied by every major central bank when dealing with their own deflating financial systems decades later.

That campaign:

1. Cut interest rates to zero (Zero Interest Rate Policy, or ZIRP).

2. Launch Quantitative Easing (QE).

I mentioned before that the BoJ burst the bubbles in Japanese stocks and real estate by aggressively raising rates from 2.5% to 6% between 1989 and mid-1990. It's important to note that this monetary tightening was as short-lived as it was aggressive: the BoJ was already *cutting* interest rates six months into 1991. By 1993, it had cut rates down to 1.75%. By 1995, rates were down to 0.5%. And in February of 1999, the BoJ took them to zero (technically 0.1%).

This marked the first time in modern history that a major central bank cut interest rates to zero. Up until this point, ZIRP was considered something of a "pipe dream" relegated to academic papers and "what if" discussions at central banks.

After all, who in their right mind believed that a country could get away with paying only 0.1% in interest to lenders for as long as two years? And what person would be willing to park his or her savings at a bank in exchange for even less than this (banks pay depositors rates that are typically lower than the official rate maintained by a country's central bank).

Well, it turns out everyone was willing to play along. There were no protests or riots. None of the policymakers who introduced ZIRP were forced to resign. And Japan's bond market didn't blow up either (more on this in a moment).

Put simply, the BoJ successfully managed to cut rates to zero without triggering a crisis. Never before had money been so cheap in Japan. So, you would expect that the economy would start growing rapidly. After all, surely Japanese businesses took advantage of these extraordinarily low rates to borrow capital and put it to productive use, thereby triggering an economic boom, right?

Wrong.

The economy didn't do anything notable. In fact, it's hard to see if ZIRP had any effect at all as far as economic growth was concerned. Below is a chart of Japan's GDP growth (year over year) from 1990 to 2010. ZIRP was introduced in 1999. See if you can determine how ZIRP made a difference.

As you can see, ZIRP was a total dud as far as economic growth was concerned. So, in March 2001, the BoJ turned to more extreme measures, namely, Quantitative Easing (QE).

Remember, we're talking about *2001* here, a full SEVEN YEARS before the Fed or any other major central bank attempted QE. The BoJ was literally in uncharted waters. And at that time in history, QE was considered the "nuclear" option as far as monetary policy was concerned.

It turned out to be a dud as well.

Chart 3: Japan Gross Domestic Product Growth Rate (1990-2010)

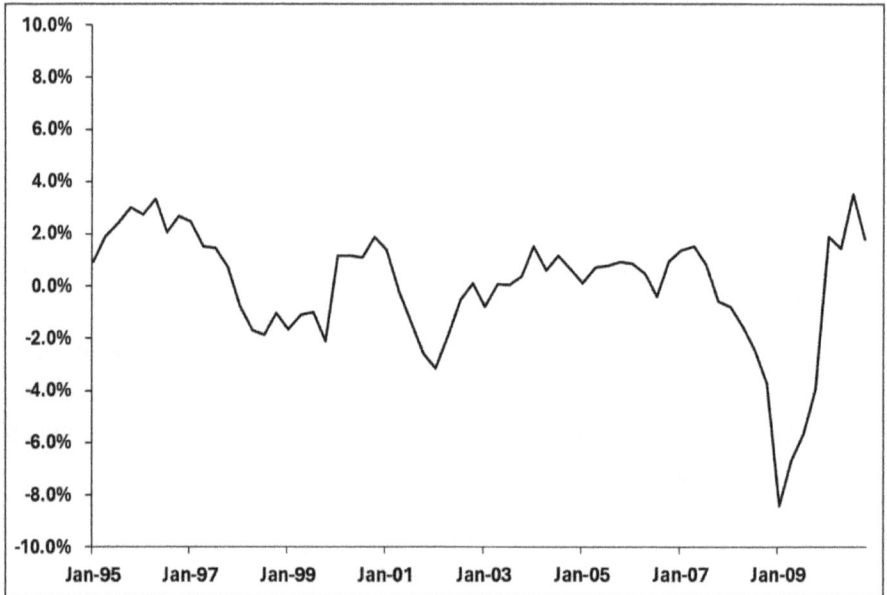

Note: Data adapted from Cabinet Office, Government of Japan [3]

As I just mentioned, the BoJ introduced QE in 2001. Return to the above chart and see if you can determine what QE accomplished as far as Japan's economy was concerned. I certainly can't see anything of note.

Central bank defenders might suggest that QE cushioned Japan's economy from a deeper economic contraction in 2008… but that is ludicrous. Why would QE do nothing for SEVEN years and then suddenly have an effect in year eight?

No, the reality is that neither ZIRP nor QE generated economic growth.

But what about job growth? Surely the BoJ's revolutionary monetary policies triggered job growth. After all, businesses could now borrow money cheaply in order to hire more people.

Wrong again. The number of people employed in Japan was ~64.6 million in 1999-2001 when ZIRP and QE were first introduced. Ten years later only ~63 million were employed.

Well, surely this is because Japan has an aging population, so the number of people working fell because many of them were retiring, right? Maybe if we account for this, we'll find ZIRP and QE actually triggered a lot of job growth for those of working age!

Wrong again. The percentage of people of working age who had jobs in Japan declined from 62% in 1999 to 59% in 2010. And if you'd like to argue that the reason it was lower in 2010 was because Japan was coming out of a recession, consider that the labor participation rate didn't actually return to 62% again until 2018.

Ok, so ZIRP and QE failed to generate economic growth... and they didn't do much of anything in terms of job creation either.

So, what exactly did these nuclear monetary policies do?

They brought yields on Japan's bonds to extreme lows. Below is a chart of the yield on the 10-Year Japanese Government bond. ZIRP and QE might not have accomplished much in terms of job creation or economic growth, but they worked incredibly well at pushing yields to extraordinary lows.

Remember, this is the yield on Japanese *Government* bonds... which represent the risk-free rate of return for Japan's financial system. So, when these yields collapsed, bond yields for other debt instruments in Japan's financial system followed.

Thus, the country's insolvent banking system and businesses were able to lurch along, albeit as debt-ridden zombies. In this sense, the BoJ's foray into monetary insanity was either a great success or a total disaster, depending on your worldview.

Chart 4: 10-Year Japan Government Bond Yield (1990-2010)

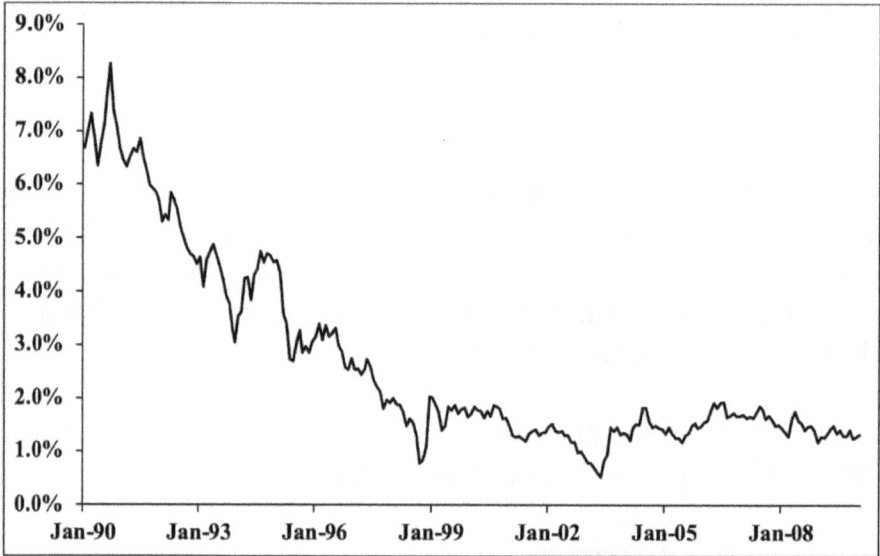

Note: Data adapted from Investing.com[4]

If you believe that the best solution to a debt problem is to prop up over-indebted businesses, thereby not letting the bad debts clear, while suppressing competition from other, better-run firms, and guaranteeing decades of weak economic growth, then the BoJ's strategy was brilliant.

If, however, you don't believe that a central bank should be supporting businesses that make bad decisions, if you think capitalism should run its course and bad businesses should go out of business, and if you prefer strong economic growth based on letting bad debts and businesses go under, then the BoJ's strategy was a **disaster**.

What's ironic, is that the man who ran the BoJ when it introduced ZIRP and QE, Masaru Hayami, was in fact **against both policies!**

A firm believer in a strong currency, Hayami thought the BoJ had no business cutting rates to zero, nor introducing QE. How ironic, then, that he will go down in history as the man who presided over the first major QE program in modern times!

Hayami's concerns aside, as far as most policymakers were concerned, ZIRP and QE were great successes. After all, it made them look like gods who could somehow magically keep an insolvent financial system chugging along.

None of the central bankers or policymakers who pushed for these policies were forced to resign, despite the clear evidence neither ZIRP nor QE really improved the economy or job market in Japan. If anything, the man who was *against* them, Masaru Hayami, was vilified by the media, while those who urged the BoJ to do more were held up as heroes!

Yes, the media applauded BoJ officials for pushing for more of the very policies that failed to create economic growth or jobs and vilified the man who was against these policies.

And so... the BoJ began a period of monetary policy insanity that would ultimately never end (more on this shortly). What initially started out as "emergency" interventions that were meant to be temporary soon became normalized. In fact, ZIRP and QE became the "go to" monetary policies for the BoJ despite the fact that those very same policies failed to solve anything in the past.

Japan wants to issue more debt to try and "spend" its way into economic growth?

Buy the debt with QE.

Japanese stocks aren't rallying anymore, and investors are getting nervous about another bear market?

Buy Japanese stocks (via funds) with QE.

QE isn't working as well as the BoJ hoped?

Expand QE by printing even more money and buying even more assets.

Even that doesn't seem to be working any longer?

You guessed it… MORE QE… and try NEGATIVE Interest Rate Policy (NIRP).

The whole mess would be hilarious if it wasn't so tragic. Japan has now experienced 20+ years of low growth as the country became ever more indebted. In the process, the BoJ effectively nationalized Japan's entire financial system.

A Slow-Motion Nationalization, 20 Years in the Making

Japan's Debt-to-GDP ratio first cleared 100% in the mid-1990s. At this level, a country is usually considered to be insolvent, meaning that it is HIGHLY unlikely it will ever pay down its debt, and bond investors start dumping the country's bonds.

This has NOT been the case for Japan.

The BoJ began interfering in its bond markets in a big way in the late '90s/ early '00s (ZIRP in 1999 and QE in 2001). Strangely, the bonds markets have given Japan a "pass" and not just for a little while… **for well over 20 years.**

Along the way, the Bank of Japan has launched:

1. Negative interest rate policy (NIRP), through which it *charges* lenders to lend it money.

2. A single QE program equal to 25% of Japan's GDP (in 2013).

3. Unlimited QE in the form of yield control, through which it prints money and buys Japanese Government Bonds **anytime** said bonds' yields begin to rise above certain levels.

As a result of this, Japan now has a Debt-to-GDP ratio of well over 260%, and there is no sign of the BoJ stopping. If anything, the BoJ appears to be nationalizing Japan's **entire financial system.**

In 2020, the BoJ became the single largest holder of Japanese stocks in the world. All told, it owned 7% of the entire Japanese stock market and was a top 10 shareholder for over half the companies that traded on the Nikkei.

By 2022, **the BoJ owned over 50% of all of Japan's debt**. Things were so out of control that there were days in which certain Japanese Government Bonds *no longer even traded* because there were no longer active buyers and sellers; the BoJ owned everything!

But wait, it gets crazier.

As a result of buying all these assets, the BoJ's balance sheet became larger than Japan's total annual economic output (GDP) in 2018. It has since grown to over 130% of Japan's GDP.

I realize that it is difficult to picture this. After all, Japan is a foreign country with a foreign currency and foreign markets. So, let's "translate" this to the U.S. and its economy.

If the Fed were to repeat what the BoJ has accomplished, its balance sheet would be over $29 TRILION in size and it would be printing $2+ trillion worth of new money every year and using it to buy assets. And we're talking years and years of this policy even when the U.S. financial system wasn't in a crisis.

This all sounds completely ludicrous, but that's the situation in Japan today: the BoJ has effectively nationalized most of Japan's financial system, owning more of Japan's stocks and bonds than any other investor in the world.

What's even more absurd is that no major policymaker who pushed for these insane policies has ever been fired or forced to resign despite the **clear evidence** that ZIRP and QE have not and apparently *cannot* produce economic growth or jobs. Remember, at this point, Japan is over 20 years into this scheme... and it has yet to experience a meaningful economic boom of any kind.

And perhaps the craziest item of all?

Japan's financial system continues to function despite this monetary insanity.

Bond investors have yet to turn on Japan. Everyone seems to be perfectly content to lend money to Japan for as long as ten years or more in exchange for basically NOTHING (the yield on the 10-Year Japanese Government Bond has been at or near zero for decades). The same is true for stock investors who continued to actively buy and sell Japanese stocks even though the Nikkei didn't hit a new all-time high for over 30 years.

I realize I sound rather cheeky here. But I don't know any other way to address what the BoJ has accomplished. It's absolutely bananas.

However, there are two positive aspects to all of this monetary madness: aside from giving us a glimpse into the playbook other central banks would employ for dealing with future crises, Japan also provides us with a disturbing truth concerning what happens when a central bank begins to do things like QE and ZIRP.

In simple terms, the lesson from Japan is this: **once a central bank embarks on a path of extraordinary monetary policy, it can NEVER escape it.**

The Money Trap: QE Forever and Low Rates for Life

As I mentioned earlier in this chapter, the Bank of Japan (BoJ) first cut interest rates to zero in 1999. What I didn't tell you before is that when the BoJ did this, it wasn't embarking on a brief experiment with ZIRP; interest rates in Japan would never recover!

Indeed, since that time, the BoJ has *never* been able to raise rates higher than 0.5%. Please note, I'm not referring to 5% but 0.5%, **as in half of a percent**.

Put another way, **once the BoJ cut rates to zero, rates would stay below 1% for the next 20+ years.**

But what about QE?

Since the BoJ first introduced QE in 2001, its balance sheet has experienced only ONE period of significant shrinkage (meaning it was selling or retiring assets at a faster pace than it was buying). That period was from February 2006 to June 2007 when the BoJ's balance sheet shrank by 33%.

Put another way, in over 20 years, there was only a single period during which the BoJ engaged in a serious attempt to normalize its balance sheet. And that period lasted only ~14 months. And since the BoJ abandoned that attempt, its balance sheet has grown five-fold!

Again, the big lesson from Japan is that once a central bank embarks on a path of extraordinary monetary policy, it can NEVER escape it.

"Now hold up a minute, Graham," you're no doubt thinking. *"Are you telling me that the Fed won't ever be able to raise rates to historical averages? So, the days of earning 3% or 5% on my bank account deposits are gone forever?"*

No. I'm not saying that. I'm saying that the Fed won't be able to raise rates to 5% and keep them there for a prolonged period of time without blowing up entire segments of the financial system… which will ultimately lead to the Fed being forced to abandon its hopes of policy normalization (more on this later in this book).

If you think that I'm delusional to believe this, consider that the Fed has already had one failed attempt at policy normalization in the last 10 years. And not only did this attempt fail, but it failed miserably: the corporate debt market froze, and the U.S. stock market crashed.

You might have missed this mess, as it occurred over the holidays in 2018. But it did happen. And bear in mind, going into that situation, the Fed wasn't engaged in anything like the monetary insanity it employed during the covid pandemic!

So, let's take a trip down memory lane and find out what happens when an overconfident Fed attempts to normalize monetary policy after a prolonged period of extreme monetary easing. This lesson will come in handy as we delve into the Fed's current attempt to end inflation later in this book.

A New Fed Chair and a New Focus For the Fed

As I write this in 2024, the current Fed Chair is Jerome Powell.

Powell was originally nominated to the position by former-President Trump in late 2017. He was sworn in as Fed Chair in February 2018. He's since procured a second term courtesy of President Joe Biden in

2021. But for now, we'll be focusing on the "Trump years" of Powell's Fed leadership.

President Trump's selection of Powell was notable for many reasons. The most significant one was that the President opted not to give the previous Fed Chair Janet Yellen a second term, but instead opted to nominate a new Fed Chair. This marked a significant departure from historical precedent in that the prior three Fed Chairs (Paul Volcker, Alan Greenspan, and Ben Bernanke) all served two full terms.

Obviously, the President wanted a change. And the change appeared to be based on private-sector credentials and professional focus: Powell, unlike Yellen, had considerable private-sector experience. Yellen was a career academic. Powell was a career businessman who had accrued a fortune of over $100 million working in private equity and banking.

Based on this, it appeared that the Trump administration wanted the Fed to move away from its focus on the financial markets (a hallmark of the Yellen and Bernanke years) to focus more on the real economy. This seemed at odds with President Trump's obsession with the stock market, but then again, many things were odd about the Trump administration and its hires for key positions.

Prior to Jerome Powell taking the helm at the Fed, the Fed had engaged in a decade of the most extraordinary monetary easing in its 105-year history. Because the Fed's policy response to the 2020 pandemic was so extreme, it's easy to forget that prior to then, it was truly extraordinary for the Fed to keep interest rates at zero for a prolonged period, let alone engage in QE. So, with that in mind, it's worth reviewing the monetary landscape Jerome Powell inherited as Fed Chair.

Between 2008 and 2018, the Fed raised interest rates a total of five times: once each in 2015 and 2016, then three times in 2017. For those of you who don't follow Fed policy I have to tell you that this represents an extraordinarily SLOW pace of monetary tightening. During a typical tightening cycle, the Fed will raise rates three or more times in a single year (this was the case in 1994, 1999, 2004, 2005, 2006, etc.).

Moreover, in 2018, the Fed had just finished printing over $3 trillion via Quantitative Easing (QE) programs. Bear in mind, the National Bureau of Economic Research (NBER) had determined that the 2008 recession was over by **mid-2009**.

Put another way, the Fed ran QE programs practically non-stop from 2009 through 2014, printing over $2 trillion, while also keeping interest rates at zero, despite the fact the U.S. economy was *technically* in recovery.

So, when Jerome Powell took the helm at the Fed, he was inheriting a central bank that had just completed what was easily its longest, most aggressive easing cycle in history up until that point.

Powell sought to completely reverse this and normalize Fed policy.

This meant raising interest rates from ~1% (where they were when he took over at the Fed) to 4%-5%. It also meant attempting to shrink the Fed's balance sheet from $3.5 trillion down to ~$1 trillion (its original size prior to the Great Financial Crisis).

Now, you would think that after 10 years of the loosest monetary policy in history, Powell would opt to *ease into* normalization. After all, by this point in time the U.S. financial system had grown quite accustomed to low interest rates, QE, and minimal if any hawkishness from the Fed.

You would be wrong.

From the very start, Jerome Powell made it clear he believed the Fed should focus on the economy, not the financial markets. And under his leadership, the Fed embarked on what was arguably its most aggressive tightening of monetary policy in history (at that point, anyway).

In 2018, the Fed raised rates FOUR times. Bear in mind, it had only performed five rate hikes in the preceding **10 years.**

However, the Powell Fed didn't just raise rates, it also began shrinking the Fed's balance sheet via a process called Quantitative Tightening (QT). This consists of the Fed allowing the debt securities it owns to reach maturity, at which point the Fed receives the cash it had loaned out. The Fed then transfers those funds to the U.S. Treasury, thereby reducing liquidity in the financial system.

Here again, the Powell Fed didn't ease into things.

The Fed first launched QT when Janet Yellen was Fed Chair in 2017. At that time the Fed implemented the program at a pace of $10 billion per month: $6 billion in Treasuries and $4 billion in Mortgage-Backed Securities or MBS.

This pace would increase at a rate of $6 billion in additional Treasuries and $4 billion in additional MBS every three months until it topped out at $30 billion worth of Treasuries and $20 billion worth of MBS, or $50 billion total every month.

The point I'm making here is that the pace of QT was already laid out *before* Jerome Powell took over at the Fed. But once he assumed the helm as Fed Chair in February 2018, he was responsible for steering this process.

Moreover, we must remember that prior to this the Fed had never engaged in QT in any meaningful way… let alone QT while also raising rates. So, it is reasonable to assume the Fed would be open to tweaking things based on market conditions.

It didn't.

The Fed Ignores Multiple Signals of Financial Distress

The Powell Fed went full steam ahead with QT increasing from $10 billion per month in October 2017 to $20 billion per month in February 2018, then $30 billion per month in May 2018 and onwards. By the time August of 2018 rolled around, **the Fed was on pace to drain an amount of liquidity equal to the size of Sweden's GDP every 12 months.**

And it nearly blew up the markets in the process.

The first sign of trouble showed up in March 2018. At that time the share prices of numerous companies that are closely aligned with the real economy began to roll over and collapse. Specifically, the largest copper producer in the U.S. (Freeport McMoran), one of the largest producers of heavy machinery (Caterpillar) and one of the largest producers of industrial and consumers goods (3M) all peaked around this time and began to nosedive.

Now, it's not unusual for a stock to peak and decline. After all, individual stocks fall all the time without it being notable. However, what *is* notable is for multiple stocks from *different sectors* all closely aligned to the *real economy* to suddenly peak and begin to collapse at the same exact time. **Anyone with a decent amount of experience monitoring the financial markets would have caught this.**

I certainly did. The Fed didn't. Despite the clear warnings that the markets were reacting negatively to the pace of QT and rate hikes, the Fed continued to increase both throughout 2018.

Now, you could argue that it wasn't the Fed's job to track individual stocks. Sure, Fed officials were routinely citing stock levels and valuations as indicating frothy sentiment during media interviews at that time… but according to the Fed's official mandates as set out by Congress, the Fed's interest in stocks should be solely tied to maintaining financial stability and nothing else.

So, to be fair, we could *technically* argue that it's not the Fed's job to catch a stock market shift like the one that occurred in February/March 2018. However, it is 100% the Fed's job to watch U.S. government bonds, or Treasuries. And by the middle of 2018, **Treasury bonds were flashing a major warning sign.**

If you'll recall from *The Everything Bubble,* the 10-year U.S. Treasury is the single most important bond in the world. The yield on the 10-Year U.S. Treasury bond is considered the "risk free rate of return" for most of the U.S. financial system: practically every risk asset you can list (stocks, commodities, real estate, etc.) is valued based on this bond's yield…

Chart 5: 10-Year United States Treasury Yield (1983-2018)

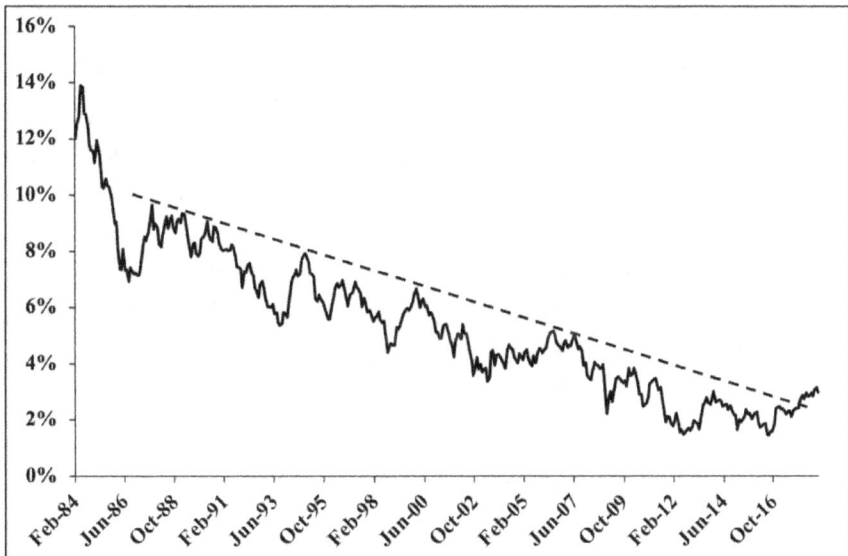

Note: Data adapted Investing.com[5]

… which is why the Fed *should* have noticed that its rate hikes and QT had resulted in **the yield on the 10-Year U.S. Treasury spiking to the point of breaking a 20+year downtrend.**

This is a *major* issue. The Fed's primary mandate is to maintain financial stability. And for a debt-based financial system such as the one the U.S. has maintained since leaving the Gold Standard in 1971, Treasury yields are one of, if not THE, most important signal of financial stability (or lack thereof).

When bond yields rise, it's because bond prices are falling. Bond prices can fall for any number of reasons, but when they fall far enough that a multi-decade bull market in bonds is ending, **it's a major concern.**

Now, some of you are no doubt wondering, *"why does this matter? After all, any publicly traded security can rise or fall anytime. The stock market routinely drops 5% and people argue that investors should buy the dip!"*

With debt, a drop in price is a BIG deal because when bond prices fall, bond yields RISE. And a higher bond yield can be indicative of **greater risk**. And remember, we are not just talking about any debt here, we are talking about U.S. Treasuries: the senior-most asset class in our current financial system!

So, when the yield on the 10-Year U.S. Treasury broke its 20+ year downtrend in 2018, the bond market was effectively saying, *"lending money to the US Government for 10 years is a LOT riskier than it was before."*

And THAT should have gotten the Fed's attention… particularly when you consider the implications of this.

A Debt-to-GDP Ratio of 100%... or Why Higher Yields Were (and Still Are) a Problem For the U.S.

As everyone knows, the U.S. has had a debt problem for decades.

What many *don't* know is that in order to sustain its mountain of debt, the U.S. must continuously issue *new debt*.

This consists of...

a. Rolling over maturing debt into new debt for pre-existing debt holders (as opposed to paying them back),

or...

b. Issuing new debt to new buyers.

When the yield on the 10-Year U.S. Treasury began to spike higher in 2018, it didn't just mean that U.S. debt was potentially *riskier*, it also meant that going forward, when the US government went to issue new 10-Year Treasuries, it would have to do so at a higher yield.

That might not be a big deal for a country with little debt (say a Debt-to-GDP ratio of 60% of lower). But in 2018, the U.S. Debt-to-GDP ratio was over 100%. At that debt level, higher yields on U.S. Treasuries meant potentially *serious issues* for the U.S. in terms of financing its debt payments.

"But wait a minute, Graham," you're probably thinking, *"you previously told me that Japan managed to function just fine with a Debt-to-GDP ratio of 260%."*

Yes, that is true. But it was only possible because Japan's central bank, the BoJ, was running QE programs almost the entire time during which Japan increased its debts levels. As I mentioned earlier in this chapter, those QE programs didn't generate economic growth or create jobs, but they did stop Japanese bond yields from spiking.

By way of contrast, in 2018 when the U.S.' Debt-to-GDP ratio was over 100%, the Fed was no longer performing QE. It was performing QT. Moreover, the Fed was raising interest rates at the same time! In this context, there was no "lid on yields" courtesy of a major Fed program. So, the spike in yields induced by this monetary tightening was indeed worrisome.

I cannot claim to know what Fed Chair Powell was thinking at that time. Perhaps he believed that the U.S. economy would start growing rapidly and the country would be able to pay down enough debt to reduce its Debt-to-GDP to more reasonable levels.

Or perhaps there is some truth to the claim that the Fed, like most of the D.C. establishment, hated President Trump and wanted to intentionally damage the economy to ruin his chances of a second term.

Or perhaps the Fed isn't composed of economic geniuses, but by people who simply make monetary policy up on the fly until something breaks!

Speaking of which…

This situation wasn't just problematic for the U.S. Treasury market. Remember, as I wrote a few paragraphs ago, Treasury yields represent the "risk free" rate for the **entire financial system**.

So, if it becomes RISKIER to lend money to the U.S. government, this will have a ripple effect on all other assets in the financial system, particularly in the secondary debt markets: corporate debt, municipal debt, etc.

Now, in terms of risk profile, it is generally riskier to lend money to a city or state, than it is to lend money to the federal government. And it is even riskier to lend money to a corporation than it is to a city or state.

I realize this can be hard to visualize, so the grading for U.S. debt from safest to riskiest is as follows:

1. Lending money to Uncle Sam (U.S. Treasuries).

2. Lending money to a municipality (a town, county, or state).
   a. Investment-grade municipalities (those with higher credit ratings).
   b. High-yield municipalities (those with lower credit ratings)

3. Lending money to a corporation.
   a. Investment-grade corporations (those with higher credit ratings).
   b. High-yield corporations (those with lower credit ratings)

As you would imagine, when things start to go south in the U.S. debt markets, the trouble first starts in the riskiest areas: high-yield corporate bonds.

That is precisely what happened in late 2018. And it was 100% the fault of the Fed. Fed leadership should have noticed what was happening in Treasuries and tweaked the QT program or altered the pace of rate hikes.

They didn't.

Despite the clear and obvious warnings from Treasury yields, the Fed continued to raise interest rates while simultaneously increasing the pace of its QT program. By the time December of 2018 rolled around, QT was $50 billion per month, and the Fed was about to implement its fourth rate hike of the year (its 7th in two years).

Then the junior debt markets blew up.

The Debt Markets Freeze and the Stock Market Crashes

The first sign of trouble hit the high-yield corporate bond market.

These are effectively bonds for companies that are at high risk of potential default even under *good* conditions. As a result of this, they are commonly referred to as "junk bonds." And they act as the proverbial "canary in the coal mine" for the debt markets in that they are the first to collapse when there's serious trouble afoot.

Junk bonds were already breaking down in September 2018 after the Fed raised rates for the third time that year and QT hit $40 billion per month. However, once the Fed raised rates in December, things started to get REALLY ugly. Between December 1st 2020 and January 10th 2021, **not a single new junk-bond issuance was completed.**

As I've been claiming for pages now, the Fed was 100% at fault for this. By this point the Fed had somehow missed the following signs of distress in the financial system:

1. Multiple stock market sectors with close ties to the real economy peaking and beginning to collapse (February-March 2018).

2. U.S. Treasury yields rising rapidly, signifying that the 20+ year bull market in bonds was ending (July-September 2018).

3. High-yield corporate bonds collapsing (October-November 2018).

4. Stocks breaking down, losing 11% of their total value in a single month (October-November 2018).

5. The high-yield corporate bond market freezing (December 1st 2018).

Despite all of the above items, the Fed still raised rates for a fourth time that year on December 20th, 2018. That's when the stock market crashed. And I do mean *crashed*: the S&P 500 nose-dived by 11% in the span of a few weeks. Individual stocks fell even further!

The situation was so ugly that then-Treasury Secretary Steve Mnuchin interrupted his Christmas holiday to publicly announce phone calls with the CEOs of the U.S.'s six largest banks as well as the President's Working Group (the famed Plunge Protection Team whose job it is to stop market crashes from happening).

This was akin to the most powerful financial insiders in the world declaring, *"DON'T PANIC! We're fixing this mess!"*

Then, and only then, did the carnage end.

And so, the Fed learned a crucial lesson... one that the Bank of Japan (BoJ) had learned 15 years before... **that once a central bank embarks on a path of extraordinary monetary policy, it can NEVER normalize.**

I want to be clear here.

It's not that a central bank won't *try* to normalize things; the BoJ, the Fed and every other major central bank that has engaged in extraordinary monetary policy has tried, sometimes multiple times, to normalize monetary policy. But, at best, their efforts last about 14 months before something breaks and they're forced to pause or even start easing again.

In the case of the BoJ, as I mentioned earlier in this chapter, there was only one significant period during which it attempted to normalize policy in the last 20 years: **from February 2006 to June 2007 (14 months).**

Since that time, the BoJ has expanded its balance sheet by 500%. And as of early-2024, short-term interest rates in Japan are still NEGATIVE.

As for the Fed, it managed to draw out its monetary policy normalization attempt to 36 months… primarily because it initially took its sweet time raising rates with only one rate hike in 2015 and 2016 each.

However, once the Fed got serious about normalizing policy and started raising rates three to four times a year while also shrinking its balance sheet, **it only took about 14 months for something to "blow up," forcing the Fed to abandon its plans.**

And so, to recap, the "Lessons from Japan" are:

- Once a central bank introduces extraordinary monetary easing, it is never able to truly normalize policy again.

- Every serious attempt at normalizing monetary policy lasts roughly 14 months before something "breaks" and the central bank is forced to abandon or alter its plans.

- Once a central bank is forced to abandon its plans for normalizing monetary policy, there isn't much time before it's back to easing again.

As I write this in early-2024, the markets are once again learning the above lessons the hard way.

The Fed has once again created a major problem (inflation) courtesy of extraordinary monetary policy. Once again, the Fed ignored the problem for too long until it became a systemic issue. Once again, the Fed began frantically trying to normalize monetary policy (rapid rate hikes and QT).

And once again, the Fed's efforts only lasted about 14 months before something started to break: three of the largest bank failures in U.S. history occurred in 2023. And the Fed has since been engaged in a back-door bailout.

Welcome to the greatest monetary screw-up of all time.

CHAPTER 3

The Greatest Monetary Screw-up of All Time

THE FED HAS made several major screw-ups during my lifetime.

It failed to identify the Tech Bubble in the late '90s.

It failed to regulate the OTC derivatives market in the late '90s/ early '00s, which set the stage for the Great Financial Crisis in 2008.

It failed to identify the Housing Bubble in the early '00s.

It failed to use the Great Financial Crisis to clear bad debts out of the financial system in '08-'11.

It failed to even *attempt* to normalize monetary policy throughout 2011-2017 when doing so would have resulted in less damage to the economy and financial system.

However, nothing, and I mean *nothing* compares to what the Fed did from mid-2020 to early 2022 when it ran EMERGENCY-LEVEL monetary easing for 20 straight months **AFTER** the recession associated with the pandemic ended.

If you'll recall, to combat the effects of the economy being shut down in 2020, the Fed:

1. Introduced Zero Interest Rate Policy (ZIRP) again.

2. Introduced "unlimited" QE which it used to buy:
   - Mortgage-Backed Securities (MBS).
   - U.S. Treasuries.
   - Corporate debt issued by corporations.
   - Corporate debt-related ETFs (stock funds linked to corporate debt).
   - Municipal debt (debt issued by states, counties, and cities).
   - Certificates of Deposit (CDs).
   - Student Loans.
   - Auto Loans.

Now, I've been extremely critical of the Fed in the past. But I want to be clear here: I don't have an issue with any of the items in the above list. I would never argue that the Fed *shouldn't* have intervened when the financial system began imploding in 2020. The alternative (full-scale collapse) would have been far too disastrous.

What I *do* have an issue with is the fact that the Fed maintained these policies **for 20 months AFTER the crisis was over**, thereby unleashing an inflationary storm.

According to the National Bureau of Economic Research (NBER), the recession triggered by the shutdowns ended in mid-2020. And yet, the Fed maintained ZIRP and its unlimited QE programs until **March 2022**.

Well, to be fair, the QE program wasn't "unlimited" after June 2020. From that point onward, the Fed was printing "just" $120 billion per month or ~$4 billion per day. And bear in mind, at that pace, this was still the Fed's largest open-ended QE program in history.

Setting aside any kind of advanced economic theory, basic common sense suggests it isn't a great idea to continue printing $120 billion per month ($1.4 trillion per year) while also keeping interest rates at zero for 20-odd months after a recession ends.

"Wait a minute, Graham," you're probably thinking, *"the U.S. had never shut down its economy before. The Fed needed to provide a lot of support to help get things back on track."*

Ok, I'll admit these were unprecedented times. But the unemployment rate was already below 6% by May of 2021. To put that into perspective, it's actually lower than the unemployment rate in 2012-2014 when the Fed was running an $80 billion-per-month QE program. So, at the very least, the Fed should have begun tapering QE in late 2020.

Unemployment was not the only metric that was on the mend either. The economy had already swung back into positive territory by the end of 2020. Indeed, by the end of the first quarter of 2021, GDP growth was above the pace it had maintained from 2010-2019. Here again, the Fed had previously run an $80 billion per month QE program in 2012-2014, at a time when GDP growth was LOWER!

I have no issue with the Fed using NUCLEAR monetary policy to stop the crisis triggered by the economic shutdowns. What I *do* have an issue with is that the Fed maintained emergency levels of monetary easing for 20 months AFTER the crisis ended… particularly when you consider that both unemployment and GDP growth were at better levels than they had been back in 2012-2014 when the Fed was running an $80 billion-per-month QE program.

There was no reason for this! The Fed should have been tapering QE and raising interest rates at the end of 2020. It didn't. Instead, it kept rates at zero and continued to print money at a pace of $1.4 TRILLION per year.

By doing this, the Fed unleashed the worst bout of inflation in 40 years.

Shutdowns + $11 TRILLION in Money Printing = An Inflationary Storm

As I noted in Chapter 1, an economy is not like a light switch that you can simply turn off and then on again without major consequence.

This is particularly true in a globalized economy, in which producing a finished good requires dozens, if not hundreds of suppliers many of which are in different countries, if not different continents.

Heck, even something as straightforward as cement requires literally *dozens* of ingredients that must be sourced. And depending on where a supplier is located, how badly covid hit the economy, and whether that country's policymakers chose to implement shutdowns, all had a major impact on the production of various raw materials and supplies.

Put simply, because of the pandemic, the world experienced its first major disruption to the supply chain in decades. The result was a global supply shortage in everything from semiconductors to shipping tankers to petrochemicals.

This alone was enough to cause inflation. After all, basic economics tells us that if demand stays the same, but there is a drop in supplies, then prices will rise.

In equation form:

Normal Demand + Fewer Supplies = Higher Prices

However, supply chain issues weren't the only thing contributing to inflation. Remember, the Fed printed ~$5 TRILLION in the span of 24 months from March 2020-March 2022. And the Fed wasn't the only one printing money: the Federal Government spent over $6 trillion over the same time period.

That's $11 trillion in new money being produced in the span of two years. And because much of this money went directly *into* the economy via stimulus checks and social spending, it had a major inflationary impact.

To top it off, the pandemic also altered consumer behavior. With everyone scared that they might not live long enough to reach retirement, and forbidden from going to public places, many Americans opted to make "dream" purchases. After all, if you can't go on vacation due to the shutdowns, why not buy the high-end fridge/swimming pool/home theater system you've been eyeing for months?

And so, courtesy of stimulus checks and the You Only Live Once (YOLO) mentality induced by the pandemic, consumer demand was actually HIGHER than normal for many items.

Thus, our equation changed from…

Normal Demand + Fewer Supplies = Higher Prices

To…

Greater Demand Fueled by $11 Trillion in Interventions and Stimulus + Fewer Supplies = MUCH Higher Prices.

And that, my friends, is the recipe for an inflationary storm.

Below is a chart of the official inflation measure for the U.S., the Consumer Price Index or CPI. Even a 3rd grader could look at that and tell you that inflation was becoming a MAJOR problem as early as the spring of 2021.

Chart 6: Consumer Price Index (2010-2022)

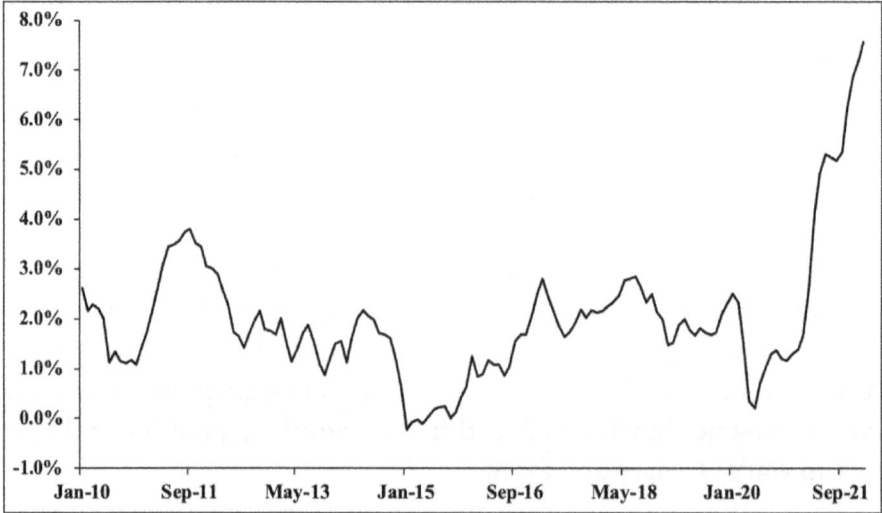

Note: Data adapted from the U.S. Bureau of Labor Statistics[6]

Unfortunately for us, the Fed was not run by 3rd graders at that time; it was run by people who *didn't* see inflation in the above chart or who lied about it. Whether it was incompetence or corruption, the Fed ignored this and many other signals that inflation was raging. Oh, and they printed another $2+ trillion in the process.

The Big Lie: Inflation is Non-Existent or Transitory

Throughout 2020 and much of 2021, the Fed claimed there was no inflation.

When that lie became too apparent, the Fed changed tactics and began claiming that there was inflation, but that it was *"transitory"* meaning it would go away by itself.

This might be the single most duplicitous thing the Fed has ever claimed.

The technical definition of the word "transitory" is *"not permanent."* So *technically*, the Fed could argue that anything, even Planet Earth, is transitory. However, for anyone who isn't interested in philosophizing about the nature of time and existence, the key concerns with any "transitory" problem are:

1. How long it lasts.

2. How much damage it causes.

In terms of the inflationary storm that hit the U.S. in late 2020/early 2021, the Fed argued that the reason the inflation data *appeared* to be rising so rapidly was because the numbers from 12 months prior (early 2020) were so abysmal due to the shutdowns.

This is called the "base effect." In economics it means that the reason your data appears a certain way is because you are comparing it to data from a previous time period (month over month, quarter of quarter, or year over year).

Let me give you an example.

Let's say that the economy is shut down and your home's value collapses 10% from $200,000 to $180,000. Then, let's say that over the course of the next 12 months, the economy turns a corner, and your home's value rises to $190,000.

Year-over-year during that second time period your home value has risen from $180,000 to $190,000 or 5%. That sounds great... except your home's value is still *down* $10,000 from its price of $200,000 prior to the shutdowns! However, an economist could still use the second set of year-over-year data to say, "home values are rising, the economy is booming!" due to the base effect.

Again, this is extremely duplicitous. And the Fed's argument that inflation was "transitory" is a truly egregious example of using the base effect to push a clearly false narrative.

To wit, throughout much of 2021, the Fed argued that the reason inflation appeared to be spiraling out of control was because the data from 2020 was so terrible due to the shutdowns that any improvement in prices made it appear as if there was a MASSIVE rise in inflation on a year-over-year basis.

Based on this line of thinking, all the Fed had to do was "wait it out" and eventually the year-over-year data would improve (2020's terrible data would be replaced by 2021's much improved data for year-over-year comparisons), and inflation would "disappear."

In the simplest of terms, according to the Fed inflation might last a year or so… but it wouldn't really cause much damage because it was largely the result of issues with the data, NOT actual prices in the real world exploding higher.

It's tempting to fall for this argument if you're an academic or beltway insider who thinks reality exists in spreadsheets as opposed to the grocery store or gas station. However, we have definitive proof that the Fed was lying through its teeth about this.

It's called the Fed's Beige Book.

The Fed's Own Research Proves It Was Lying!

If you're unfamiliar with the Fed's Beige Book, it's a report the Fed publishes eight times per year.

In it, the 12 regional banks that comprise the Federal Reserve banking system (Boston, New York, Philadelphia, Cleveland, Richmond, Atlanta, Chicago, St. Louis, Minneapolis, Kansas City, Dallas, and San Francisco), present anecdotal information on the U.S. economy. The Fed retrieves this information via interviews and conversations with business leaders, market experts and other people at the frontlines of the economy.

You can think of the Beige Book as the Fed's attempt at "outreach," through which it gives its business contacts and others the ability to tell the Fed what they are experiencing in the real world.

With that in mind, throughout 2021, captains of industry and business managers were telling the Fed that they were *extremely* worried about inflation. Emphases are added in the quotes below.

> *"businesses in most sectors expect fairly widespread increases in the prices they pay in the months ahead…"*

~Beige Book March 2021.

> *"Prices accelerated slightly since the last report, with many Districts reporting moderate price increases and some saying prices rose more robustly. Input costs rose across the board, but especially in the manufacturing, construction, retail, and transportation sectors—specifically, metals, lumber, food, and fuel prices."*

~Beige Book April 2021.

> *"Looking forward, contacts anticipate facing cost increases and charging higher prices in coming months… On balance, overall price pressures increased further since the last report."*

~Beige Book May 2021.

*On balance, **overall price pressures increased further since the last report**. Selling prices increased moderately, **while input costs rose more briskly.***

~Beige Book June 2021.

*Inflation was reported to be steady at an elevated pace, **as half of the Districts characterized the pace of price increases as strong, while half described it as moderate**... Several Districts indicated **that businesses anticipate significant hikes in their selling prices in the months ahead.***

~Beige Book September 2021.

To fully understand the implications of the above comments, we need to delve into the specifics of how inflation enters the financial system. The following section is a bit technical, so if you're content with the view that "inflation was in the financial system in 2021 and the Fed were fools to ignore it" feel free to skip ahead to the next section.

The Three Phases of Inflation

First and foremost, you need to know that inflation is in fact a very complicated thing. It's not as if the Fed or Federal Government prints money, hands it out, and POOF inflation appears.

Instead, inflation works its way into the financial system in phases. They are:

Phase 1: Price increases in raw materials
Phase 2: Price increases in factory gate prices
Phase 3: Price increases in consumer prices

In Phase 1 the price of raw materials begins to spike. This can be due to supply issues (shutdowns reduce exploration, extraction, and production) or specific political problems (many commodities are produced in areas that are unstable).

In 2020, the world economy had both supply issues *and* political problems. If someone contracted COVID-19 at a uranium mine or a steel mill, production was often halted, resulting in a significant drop in the production of raw materials. Throw in the fact that the political class was reticent to reopen the global economy, and even those raw materials that were produced were left sitting in shipping containers or trucks instead of finding their way to the factories or manufacturing plants where they were badly needed.

As a result of the above issues, the U.S. entered Phase 1 of inflation in the second half of 2020 (yes, it happened that early). Consider that by the end of 2020, the price of copper, lumber, corn, and other raw materials were well above the levels at which they had traded **prior to the lockdowns.** In fact, they were higher than the prices at which they traded in 2017, 2018, and 2019.

This was no base effect; these items were objectively MORE expensive. And bear in mind, we're talking about the end of 2020; the Fed and Uncle Sam would go on to print/ spend trillions of dollars for another 15 months!

Now, one or two months of higher commodity prices is no big deal for manufacturers because they either have fixed price contracts that were established months ago, or they hedge their costs with futures. However, once you're talking about six or more months of steadily rising prices in commodities, things get messy.

At that point manufacturers are forced to start raising the prices of finished goods or face shrinking profit margins. This is when you see Phase 2 of inflationary price hikes: Price increases in factory gate prices.

In today's economy the company that *makes* something is rarely the one that sells it to the public. Instead, manufacturers first sell their goods to retailers, who then sell the goods to the public.

Think of Wal-Mart for example. Wal-Mart doesn't actually *produce* anything. It simply buys finished goods from suppliers (2,800 of them) at what are called "factory gate prices" and then marks the items up to sell them to consumers at a profit.

Because of this, once inflation begins to really take root in the financial system, you start to see it reflected in price hikes in factory gate prices. And according to the Chicago Business Barometer, factory gate prices hit a 41-year high in April of 2021.

This means that the last time factory gate prices spiked at a similar pace was in 1980 **during one of the worst inflationary periods in history when the Fed was forced to raise rates to over 15%.**

And yet, in April of 2021 when the price of every major commodity was well above its pre-pandemic highs and factory gate prices were at 41-year highs, the Fed was still arguing adamantly that inflation was "transitory."

This was not just a public statement either. The Fed was actively printing money during this time. Indeed, it would go on to print another $1.2 trillion before it decided to take inflation seriously.

Now, factory gate prices are a bit like raw material prices in that a temporary price spike can be managed without retailers having to increase the price they are charging consumers. However, if higher factory gate prices persist, eventually retailers are forced to start raising prices or lose profitability.

Which brings us to the final phase of inflation entering the economy: Price increases in consumer prices. The U.S. entered this phase of inflation in late 2021/early 2022. At that time, corporations began preparing the public for higher prices:

Coca-Cola CEO says company will raise prices [in 2022] to offset higher commodity costs
CNBC, July 1, 2021

Disneyland Raises Ticket Prices, Adds Most Expensive Tier for Busiest Days
Bloomberg, October 24, 2021

Tesla Quietly Raises Prices on Four of Its EVs
The Verge, October 24, 2021.

Oreo cookies, Ritz crackers and Sour Patch Kids will cost more next year, Mondelez CEO says
Today.com, November 4, 2021

McDonald's Raises Menu Prices as U.S. Worker Wages Climb
NY Post January 27, 2022.

Shrinkflation: Gatorade gets a waistline and other examples of product downsizing
KHOU, March 2022.

The last headline is particularly significant. Companies don't always simply raise prices on consumer goods. Instead, they can achieve the same goal (charge more) via different strategies. One of the more common ones is to charge the **same amount for less of a finished product.**

This is called shrinkflation.

If you've ever noticed when you open a bag of chips or some other container that 30%-50% of the container is empty… that's shrinkflation in action. In that scenario, a company continues to use the same container, but simply fills it with less product and changes the print on the outside. So, while both the bag and the price are the same, you're now paying for 12oz of chips instead of 16oz.

Another example of shrinkflation is for a company to simply shrink the size of the container in which a product is being sold while maintaining the same price. *Gatorade* accomplished this in early 2022 by altering the bottles it used for its beverages to ones that had a "pinched waistline" or hour-glass figure rather than a cylinder. The result meant less *Gatorade* being sold for the same price per bottle.

You get the idea.

We've covered a lot of ground regarding inflation in the last few pages. So, I want to remind you that the reason I'm presenting the above analysis is because throughout 2021 Fed leadership claimed inflation either didn't exist or was "transitory."

When the Fed did this, it was not only ignoring its own research (the Beige Book), but it was also ignoring countless other data points (commodity prices, factory gate prices, comments by CEOs, etc.). This is truly astonishing especially when you consider that the Fed has:

1. Over 400 economics PhDs on payroll.

2. Roughly 150 research assistants on payroll.

3. Access to the best real-time economic insights before anyone else courtesy of its Beige Book research.

How did all these people, with their advanced understanding of economics, screw up their analysis of inflation so badly?

Throughout 2021 I wrote numerous research reports arguing that inflation was not transitory and that it was becoming deeply embedded in the economy. Now, I take extreme pride in the quality of my work... but I find it hard to believe that I'm somehow smarter than the collective intelligence of over 500 Fed researchers!

What was the issue here?

Was it an issue of Fed leadership playing politics and ignoring Fed researchers' work or refusing to acknowledge inflation to further a particular agenda?

Or is it true that economics PhDs have little to no understanding of real-world economics? Maybe few if any of them believed inflation was a real issue despite the countless signs?

Or perhaps Fed officials believed that the business owners telling them that their businesses anticipated *"significant hikes in their selling prices in the months ahead"* were either idiots or lying?

Whatever the case, there is literally NO EXCUSE for the Fed screwing this up as badly as it did. The Fed's purpose as laid out in its Dual Mandate is to *"foster economic conditions that achieve both stable prices and maximum sustainable employment."*

"Stable prices" is Fed speak for "little if any inflation." Unleashing the worst bout of inflation in 40 years by maintaining emergency-levels of money printing for 20 months AFTER a recession ended doesn't exactly meet those criteria.

In fact, I would argue that it was...

The Greatest Monetary Policy Screw-up of All Time

I realize I sound *extremely critical* of the Fed in these pages.

But honestly, I don't know how else to frame what the Fed did from mid-2020 to early 2022. Remember, in arguing that inflation was non-existent or "transitory" the Fed was:

1. Ignoring countless business owners' statements that inflation was a major problem as featured in the Fed's Beige Book.

2. Ignoring the price spikes in commodities.

3. Ignoring factory gate prices hitting 41-year highs.

4. Ignoring countless warnings from CEOs and other captains of industry that they would be forced to raise prices.

5. Ignoring the fact that the official inflation metric, the Consumer Price Index (CPI), had spiked to its highest level since 1990.

But wait, it gets worse.

The Fed was also ignoring the fact that home prices were rising at a faster pace than that of the Housing Bubble of the early '00s.

Home prices weren't the only item that was skyrocketing higher, either. The stock market erased its entire shutdown losses by August of 2020 and was at **new all-time highs** before the year ended!

Again, the stock market was at NEW ALL-TIME HIGHS within seven months of the economy being shut down for the first time in history. And yet, somehow the Fed didn't connect the dots and pump the brakes on its money printing.

Things only became more egregious from there.

Warren Buffet's favorite measure for valuing stocks is to compare the total stock market capitalization to U.S. GDP. Buffett famously used this metric in the late '90s to determine that the stock market was in a bubble at the time and chose to steer clear of technology stocks as a result.

At the peak of the Tech Bubble, the total stock market capitalization to GDP ratio for the U.S. was 150%. Well, this same ratio hit over 200% during the bubble the Fed created during the pandemic! And yet, the Fed somehow didn't see that things were getting out of control in the financial system!?!

I mention housing and stocks because they comprise the largest percentage of household wealth in the U.S. Because of this, the Fed *usually* pays close attention to them. But these were not the only signs that things were going "off the rails." Among the most jaw dropping...

a. Options trading volume (a sign of speculation) was exponentially higher in late 2021 than it was during the Tech Bubble.

b. Crypto currencies that were invented *as jokes* (Dogecoin) and backed by nothing were valued at $50 BILLION.

c. Tesla (TSLA), which sold ~300,000 cars in 2020, was worth more than the value of every other auto manufacturer on the planet combined.

d. People were selling Non-Fungible Tokens (NFTs) of farts, toilet paper, *New York Times* articles and more.

e. At one point, images of "bored apes" were being sold for **millions of dollars.**

f. "Meme stocks" or stocks that were traded for ironic/humorous purposes by novice traders who were stuck at home due to the lockdowns were rising thousands of percent in a matter of weeks.

g. Former President Trump's Special Purpose Acquisition Company (SPAC) rose to a value of $5 billion **despite its prospectus stating that it had no actual business or operations!?!**

How did the Fed miss this stuff?

Look, I get it… it's difficult to imagine a Fed researcher saying, *"Chairman Powell, Dogecoin is worth $50 billion, and someone just sold an NFT of a fart"* during a Fed meeting. I certainly wouldn't want to be the person telling Fed leadership about this stuff!

However, when you consider the above items, along with what commodity prices, housing prices, and the stock market were doing… not to mention month after month of rising inflation data, rising factory gate prices, rising retail prices… as well as statements made by Fortune 500 CEOs, captains of industry, and small business owners regarding price increases… I'm sure you'll agree that the Fed's screw-up regarding inflation was **arguably the greatest monetary policy screw-up of all time.**

And bear in mind, the Fed wasn't just ignoring all of the above items… it was ALSO maintaining ZIRP while printing an average of $4 billion per day or $120 billion per month throughout this time period!

Even more astonishing, $40 billion of that $120 billion per month was being used to buy mortgage-backed securities, which pushed mortgage rates to *extreme* lows. And this was at a time when home prices were rising more rapidly in value than they had done during the Housing Bubble of the '00s!

And so, once again, we had all the pieces in place for a massive bust:

- The financial system is showing clear signs of froth and/or a bubble? CHECK!

- The Fed is way behind the curve in terms of normalizing policy? CHECK!

- Everyone knows the Fed is way behind the curve to the point that the Fed is becoming something of a joke? CHECK!

Clearly this would end badly. The big question was what kind of bust it would be.

Would the Fed end inflation by ending its emergency-level QE program rapidly while simultaneously hiking rates? Sure, this would trigger a deflationary episode of sorts which would damage stocks and the economy, but at least the bond market wouldn't blow up...

... or would the Fed double down on its screw-up and fiddle while inflation raged... thereby allowing inflation to blow up stocks AND bonds?

The Fed opted for the latter choice.

The Fed Kinda Sorta Starts *Thinking* About Normalizing

Having spent most of 2021 claiming that inflation was transitory and would eventually disappear on its own, only to have that entire narrative blow up in its face, the Fed took its sweet time tightening monetary policy.

In October of 2021, the Fed announced it intended to start tapering QE.

Bear in mind, the Fed wouldn't actually taper anything until the following month (November). So, the October announcement was simply that the Fed was kinda sorta thinking about no longer printing money... while still printing $120 billion per month.

This is like stating you're kinda thinking about going on a diet, while reaching for your fifth piece of cake. Still, at least the Fed would finally take action in November 2021. Perhaps it would make up for lost time by rapidly tapering QE and implementing rate hikes!

NOPE!

In its October 2021 announcement, the Fed stated it would taper QE by just $15 billion per month. This meant that it would be another **eight months** before the Fed actually stopped printing money… at a time when inflation was already over 6% and showing no signs of slowing.

Even more astonishing, the Fed stated it wouldn't start raising rates until QE ended. So, the Fed's master plan for dealing with inflation was to keep rates at zero for at least another eight months… while printing hundreds of billions of dollars. Bear in mind, the Fed was saying this at a time when inflation, as measured by the CPI, hit 6.8% (a 40-year high).

What was the Fed thinking here? Why was it so slow to tighten monetary policy?

Perhaps Fed Chair Jerome Powell was a little gun shy after the Fed's 2018 attempt at normalizing monetary policy blew up in his face. However, that argument overlooks one glaring issue. In 2018, inflation wasn't a problem; the Fed was simply trying to normalize policy at a time when both the economy and the stock market were doing quite well!

By way of contrast, in 2021, inflation was a once-in-multiple-decades-type problem, stocks were in an obvious bubble (as was housing and multiple other asset classes) and things were rapidly spinning out of control in terms of mania (again, people were selling NFTs of farts, toilet paper, and the like).

Put simply, 2021 was NOT a time for the Fed to be cautious. The Fed needed to act decisively!

If you think I'm being overly dramatic here, consider that one month after the Fed began its feeble tapering of QE (December 2021), CPI cleared 7%. That same month, a *CNN* poll showed that 80% of Americans saw *"the rising cost of food and other everyday items"* as the single largest economic issue!

When, if ever, can you remember 80% of Americans agreeing on anything? It's rare that even 60% of us agree on a particular issue. And yet, in December 2021, 80% of Americans told a pollster that inflation was their #1 concern.

So, what did the Fed do? Did it end QE right then and there and start raising rates?

NOPE!

Following the announcement that inflation was over 7% and with practically all of America screaming that inflation was a major problem, the Fed announced it would double the pace of its QE taper to $30 billion per month and then start raising rates once it completed this process.

Put another way, the Fed told Americans, *"We hear you loud and clear... we're only going to print money for another three months and then raise rates above zero. America, consider your inflation problem SOLVED!"*

I realize it might be difficult to understand the full implications of what I'm writing here... especially if you haven't bothered thinking about inflation before (lucky you!). So let me break this down in very simple terms. Inflation is over **7%**. The Fed has rates at **0.25%**. And it has just announced it is going to print another **$300 billion before it raises rates.**

In a sane world, the Fed's entire leadership would have been fired and replaced by competent individuals. But we don't live in a sane world. We live in this world. And in this world, in late 2021, the Beltway crowd seemed to believe the Fed knew what it was doing.

Never mind that the median home price in the U.S. had hit new all-time highs every month for over 12 months straight.

Never mind that the New York Stock Exchange had almost DOUBLED from its pandemic lows and was now over 20% higher than it was BEFORE the pandemic.

And forget about the fact that the price of everything under the sun was up double if not triple digits (real inflation was much higher than 7%).

And let's also ignore the fact that everyone from Fortune 500 CEOs to schoolteachers in Ohio were screaming that inflation was a major problem (obviously these folks were part of some vast conspiracy and didn't realize the Fed had everything under control).

The Fed didn't stop printing money until March of 2022, by which time it had **printed another $300 billion, CPI was 8.5%, and the average daily gas price in the U.S. was over $4 per gallon.**

Actually, the Fed didn't stop printing money in March 2022. Between March 9th, 2022 (when QE allegedly ended) and April 14th, the Fed's balance sheet expanded by another $55 billion. So even after the Fed was supposed to stop printing money, it kept doing it.

The Fed *did* finally raise rates though, in March 2022. However, here again it eased into things with a measly 0.25% rate hike. This meant that rates were now at 0.5%-0.75% while inflation was 8.5%. Suffice to say, the Fed was behind the curve. But just how behind the curve was it?

Glad you asked!

Bonds Call the Fed's Bluff

As I outlined in my first book, *The Everything Bubble: The End Game for Central Bank Policy*, U.S. sovereign debt, called Treasuries, are the bedrock of our current financial system.

These bonds are the senior-most asset class in our financial system. And their yields represent the "risk free" rate of return against which all risk assets are valued.

This includes stocks.

Treasury yields move based on many things, including economic growth, financial conditions, and inflation. When inflation is roaring, bond investors require Treasuries to pay higher yields in order to compensate for this greater risk.

Think of it this way: let's say inflation is at 8%, and Uncle Sam says, *"I'll pay you 2% a year to lend me money."* Would you take him up on this? Heck no! You'd want Uncle Sam to pay you 8% or more, otherwise you're technically *losing money* by lending to him.

This issue doesn't just pertain to new lenders either.

In 2021 as inflation roared higher, Treasuries yields followed, resulting in Treasury bond prices collapsing (remember, Treasury prices fall when Treasury yields rise). As a result of this, those investors who were sitting on bonds they'd previously bought did what anyone who doesn't like losing money does in such a situation: they started unloading their bonds, which only forced Treasury prices LOWER and Treasury yields HIGHER.

Thus far in this book, we've mocked the Fed quite a bit, particularly for claiming that inflation was "transitory" while ignoring countless signals that this was not true. Even if we can somehow give the Fed a "pass" for ignoring other items...**there is no way the Fed should have missed what was happening in the bond markets in late 2021.**

Remember, the #1 focus for the Fed is financial stability. So, if the senior-most asset class in the financial system is flashing "DANGER!", the Fed should take note.

It didn't. Enter Exhibit #234,212 (joking) for evidence that inflation was a major problem, which the Fed ignored.

Chart 7: 2-Year United States Treasury Yield (2019-2022)

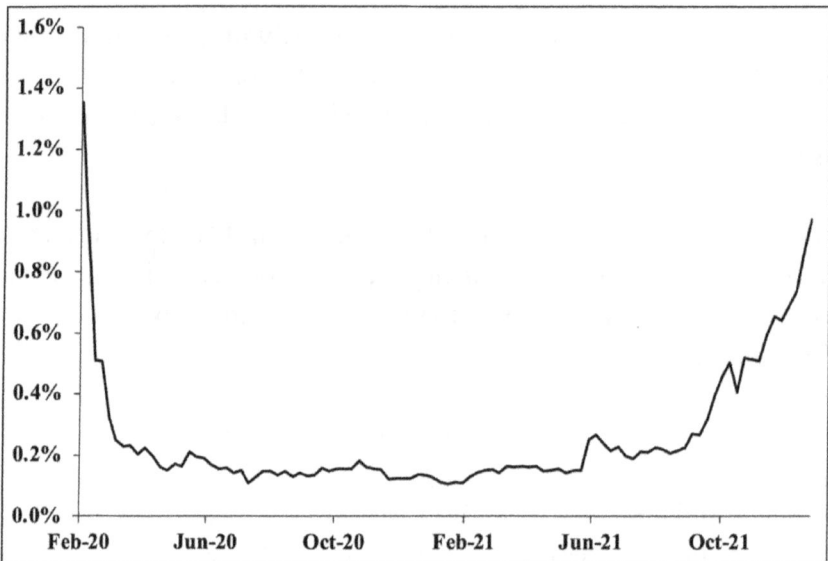

Note: Data adapted from Investing.com[7]

That is a chart of the yield on the 2-Year U.S. Treasury. It represents what investors require in terms of return to lend their capital to the U.S. government for a period of two years.

This is the bond from which the Fed takes its cues on where rates need to be. So, the fact that the yield on the 2-Year U.S. Treasury was already at 0.5% in November 2021 when the Fed still had rates at 0.25% was the equivalent of the bond market telling the Fed, *"Rates are too low, you're behind the curve on inflation."*

And yet, the Fed still kept rates at 0.25% for another FOUR months (until March 2022). By that time, the yield on the 2-Year U.S. Treasury had spiked to over 1.3%.

Put simply, during the four months the Fed sat on its hands, it went from being behind the curve by 0.25% to being behind the curve by over 1.0%. What's truly staggering to consider is that the Fed didn't *have* to do this; it could have easily raised rates at either of its FOMC meetings in November or December 2021 or at the very latest in January 2022.

It didn't.

Instead, the Fed simply *slowed* the pace of its money printing while Treasuries, the single most important asset class in our current financial system, collapsed, pushing their yields higher.

So, what did the Fed do when March 2022 finally rolled around? Did it raise rates by 0.75% to *"send a message"* to the bond markets that it was serious about stopping inflation?

NOPE!

The Fed raised rates by just 0.25% on March 17th, 2022. And it stated that it didn't intend to start shrinking its now ~$9 trillion balance sheet for several more months.

The yield on the 2-Year U.S. Treasury promptly soared to 2.6%. With rates now at 0.5%-0.7%, the Fed was now behind the curve on inflation by 1.9%. Remember, it had only been behind the curve by 1.0% a mere three weeks earlier!

Put another way, once the Fed finally got around to raising rates, it was soon **more behind the curve than it was before it had hiked rates at all!**

History will not be kind to policymakers on this. Having already committed the Mother of All Screw-ups by ignoring the mountains of evidence that inflation was a major problem as early as March 2021, the Fed then dragged its feet when it finally got around to tightening monetary policy to address this issue.

The Fed Finally Gets Serious and the Everything Bubble Finally Bursts

Having dragged its feet on tackling inflation for over a year, while printing $1+ trillion, the Fed *finally* got serious about the issue in May of 2022 when it raised rates by 0.5%.

What followed was one of the most aggressive tightening schedules in history: the Fed raised rates by 0.75% in June, July, September, and November of 2022. It followed these moves with another 0.5% rate hike in December 2022 and four 0.25% rate hikes in 2023, bringing rates from 0.25% to 5.5% in the span of 17 months.

The Fed blew up both stocks and bonds in the process (though stocks recovered most of their 2022 losses in 2023 courtesy of a back door bailout the Fed introduced in March 2023).

You likely won't read this anywhere else, but 2022 was one of the worst years for investors in history. Stocks finished the year down 20% while

Treasuries had their worst year EVER, with the long end of the yield curve falling 30%.

This is a critical point.

Historically, Treasuries have acted as hedges for stocks, as investors rush into Treasuries as a safe haven whenever the financial system goes into "risk off" mode. This was the case in 2008, when stocks lost $7.2 trillion but bonds returned $2.9 trillion.

Investors didn't have this cushion in 2022, as both stocks AND bonds collapsed. The latter asset class was the most concerning, as bonds entered their first bear market in 40 years. The below chart needs no explanation. The downtrend for bond yields ended in 2022 for the first time since the early 1980s.

Chart 8: 10-Year United States Treasury Yield (1983-2022)

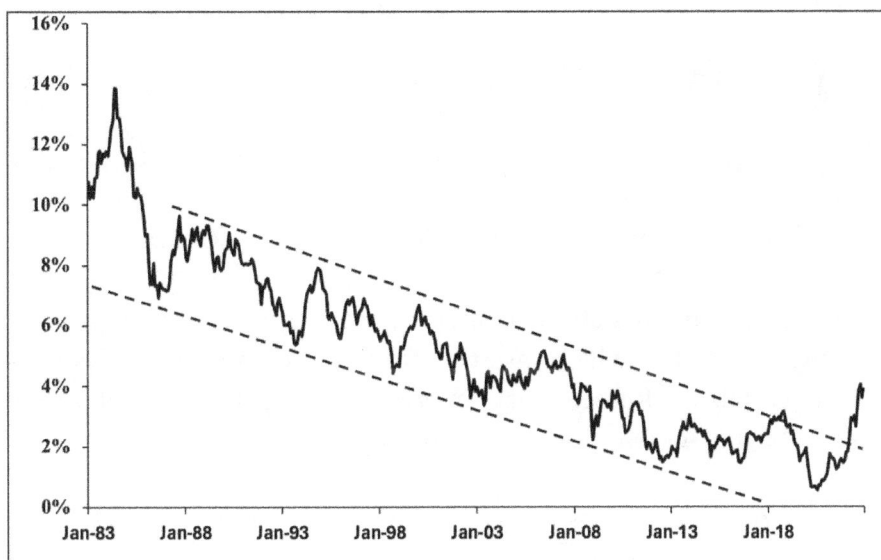

Note: Data adapted from Investing.com[5]

It is difficult to explain the significance of this.

The defining characteristic for the financial system during the 40 years from 1982 to 2022 was the bull market in bonds. When bonds are in a bull market, bond prices rise, and bond yields FALL. This means that it becomes *cheaper* to issue debt.

So, in the simplest of terms, the bull market in bonds from 1982 until 2022 represented a 40-year period in which it became cheaper and cheaper for everyone from the Federal Government to Fortune 500 companies to small businesses and even individual Americans to take on debt.

And remember, the yield on Treasuries also represents the risk-free rate of return against which all asset classes (real estate, stocks, etc.) are priced. It is not coincidence that housing, stocks, and other risk assets all experienced one of the greatest periods of wealth creation in history from 1982 to 2022.

That period ended in 2022. And it may not come back for years, if not decades.

The World of Money is Now Much More Complicated

Please understand, my above analysis isn't meant to indicate that we're entering a period in which investors are doomed to non-stop losses as risk assets collapse. Rather, what I'm saying is that going forward, investing will be much more complicated.

Consider the implications of higher short-term rates for the American public.

For some people (the wealthy), the rise in rates triggered by inflation and the Fed's monetary tightening has been highly beneficial as they (the wealthy) can now earn considerably more interest income risk-free.

When yields were at 0.25%, the person with $1,000,000 in the bank was making just $2,500 in interest income per year. However, with six-month T-bills yielding ~5%, that same person can collect $50,000 in interest on his or her cash in a year. That's an additional $47,500 in discretionary income for this person per year (~$4000 per month) without working a single hour… or touching his or her cash pile.

By way of contrast, for anyone who doesn't have large amounts of capital (the lower 70%-80% of the economy), the rise in rates has meant higher credit card payments, higher mortgage payments, etc. For these individuals, the rise in rates, combined with higher inflation, has been disastrous.

Things are also more complicated from an investing perspective.

For years, stocks were in what was called the "TINA" trade, meaning "There Is No Alternative." What this meant was that if you wanted capital appreciation or interest income you had to invest in stocks because Treasuries were offering almost nothing (sub-1% on the short-end of the yield curve).

Not anymore.

Bonds are now providing significant returns (4%+ for the entire yield curve out to 30 years) for those with money to invest. As a result of this, stocks must produce much higher returns in order to justify the additional risk they have as an asset class.

After all, why risk owning an asset class that historically returns 9% a year but can lose 20%-30% in a month or even a week (stocks), when you can own the equivalent of "cash" (short-term Treasuries or Money Market Funds) and earn 5% per year practically risk free?

The result of this will be greater volatility in stocks as investors are more "trigger happy" about getting in and out of the asset class. So, I expect plenty of nose-dives in stocks as well as plenty of "rip your face off" rallies. Navigating this situation will be MUCH more difficult than most of the last 20 years.

Things are more complicated in the work force as well.

Remember how I mentioned that bonds have been in a bull market since 1982? Well one of the implications of this is that multiple generations of Wall Street analysts, hedge fund managers, bank executives, etc. **have gone their entire careers without experiencing a bear market in bonds or a period of higher inflation.**

Put it this way, if you were managing money during the last period of major inflation in the 1970s, you are currently in your 60s, if not your 70s. Historically, Wall Street is a young man's profession (the average age on Wall Street today is mid-20s). So, unless someone REALLY loves finance/investing, odds are that those executives or fund managers who were active in the 1970s are now retired.

The consequence of this is that few if any people who are managing large pools of capital (or banks) today have any real-world experience with inflation or a bear market in bonds. It's one thing to have investing models that tell you what to do when T-bills yield 5%, **it's something else entirely to be actively managing money in that environment.**

The flipside of this is that everyone, and I do mean EVERYONE, is accustomed to how things have been for the last 50 years. Heck, the average Wall Street analyst began his or her career AFTER the Great Financial Crisis of 2008! So not only are these people inexperienced as far as inflation goes, but they think things like Zero Interest Rate Policy (ZIRP), Quantitative Easing (QE), and the Fed backstopping everything are normal.

We are seeing the consequences of this playing out in the banking sector already with three of the largest bank failures in U.S. history occurring in 2023 (Silicon Valley Bank, Signature Bank, First Republic Bank).

The reason for these bank failures?

Their management teams failed to prepare their bond portfolios for higher rates. Bear in mind, once the Fed started raising rates in March 2022, it was adamant that it wouldn't stop doing so until inflation was brought back to its target of 2%.

So, it's pretty stunning to think that the folks running some of the largest banks in the U.S. didn't take steps to prepare their bond/loan portfolios for higher rates despite the Fed stating time and again that it would be raising rates. This is akin to standing on train tracks, hearing a train in the distance, and choosing NOT to move.

Again, multiple generations of executives and fund managers have gone their entire lives in a different environment than the one we are in now. The learning curve is going to be steep for many of them as well as for those investors entering the markets now as young adults.

There are many more implications for the bear market in bonds, but you get the general idea with the above examples: things are now much more complicated in the economy and the financial system. And nowhere is it more problematic than with the Federal Government.

It's Now MUCH More Expensive for the U.S. to Service Its Debt

As I write this in early 2024, the yield on the 3-Month U.S. Treasury is 5.5%.

The last time the yield on this bond was anywhere near this level was in 2007. And before that you'd have to go back to 2001 for this bond to yield this much.

However, things were VERY different for Uncle Sam's finances at those periods in history. The U.S. had ~$10 trillion and $5-6 trillion in debt in 2007 and 2001, respectively. Today it has over $33 trillion in debt and a Debt-to-GDP ratio of 120%. As a result of this, these high Treasury yields are much more problematic today.

Let me give you an example.

On May 24th 2023, the U.S. Treasury issued $43 billion in 5-year Treasuries. Based on where the yield on the 5-Year Treasury was trading in 2020 or 2021, Uncle Sam would have paid just 0.5% or $215 million in interest payments per annum if it had issued this same amount in 5-Year Treasuries during those years. In 2023, because of the rise in yields brought about by inflation and the Fed's monetary tightening, **the U.S. will be paying $1.6 BILLION per year to service this debt.**

That's a near SEVEN-FOLD increase in debt servicing costs.

And bear in mind, we're talking about just one bond here! This dynamic is playing out across the entire yield curve. As a result of this, net interest payments on the U.S.' debt have increased from $352 billion in 2021 to $659 billion in 2023. And they're expected to clear $1 trillion shortly.

Will this trigger a crisis soon? I don't know. What I do know is that the only reasons the U.S. was able to amass so much debt over the last 20 years were:

1. Bond yields were low.

2. The Fed was engaged in large-scale QE programs.

The first of these is now over. It's possible that bond yields will return to extraordinary lows at some point in the future, but it would take a crisis/recession to cause this. And that's assuming that all future crises/ recessions play out as they have in the last 25 years which isn't a guarantee: historically there have also been inflationary recessions in which inflation *didn't* disappear and bond yields remained high (see the 1970s).

Moreover, it's not clear that the Fed really has what it takes to end inflation. Sure, Fed officials talk tough about inflation in public, but those same people advocated for pumping over $400 billion in liquidity into the financial system in the span of three weeks as soon as a handful of politically connected banks got into trouble in 2023.

Moreover, even if the Fed IS serious about insuring inflation disappears, its efforts are being thwarted by the U.S. government's fiscal policy: as I write this, the U.S. is running a $1.6 trillion deficit at a time when the economy is still growing! To put that into perspective, it's the largest deficit as a percentage of GDP in history outside of WWII.

All of that spending and debt issuance is highly inflationary.

This brings us to the second reason why the U.S. was able to amass so much debt in the last 20 years: the Fed was engaged in large-scale QE programs. Here again, the macro landscape has changed dramatically. For one thing, it's not clear that the Fed could introduce another round of large-scale QE without triggering a resurgence in inflation. Sure, Japan was able to do this for 20+ years, but that was because inflation hadn't already appeared in the global financial system during that time.

It has now.

So again, things are much more complicated in the financial system today. To be blunt, I have no idea how all of this will play out. No one does. There are far too many moving parts and too many unknowns:

government spending, economic growth, debt servicing costs, inflation, Treasury yields, Fed policy, etc.

While I don't have a clear forecast for how this plays out, what I *do* have is a clear framework for understanding how the Fed operates. I also know that egregious money printing is now politically toxic courtesy of inflation. This means that the Fed will have to approach things differently when something breaks and the next crisis hits.

Welcome to the Future of Monetary Policy.

CHAPTER 4

The Future of Monetary Policy

THUS FAR IN this book we've detailed two important truths concerning policymakers and the policies they employ.

Those truths are:

1. Once a central bank embarks on a path of extraordinary monetary stimulus and interventions, there is no going back: monetary policy can never normalize.

2. The fiscal and monetary policies employed by policymakers in response to the pandemic gave us the blueprint for how they will deal with all future crises: by printing money and funneling it into the financial system and economy via the buying of assets and stimulus checks, respectively.

Putting these two truths together, we now have a framework for predicting what will happen when this current business cycle turns and the inevitable bust hits.

That framework is as follows:

1. Something will "break" in the financial system and/or the economy will enter a recession. Either or both developments will trigger deflation in risk assets (stocks, real estate, etc.) that will become headline news.

    That last point is key; there are ALWAYS problems in the economy and the financial markets. However, for something to warrant a major policy response, it needs to enter the public's consciousness. At that point, we proceed to #2.

2. Policymakers will deal with this problem by introducing monetary policies and stimulus programs that are more extreme than those they used to combat the previous crisis.

    These responses will break into two categories.

    a. More extreme versions of previously used policies (deeper interest rate cuts, larger QE programs).

    b. Policies that are unprecedented: buying assets that are technically outside the Fed's mandate, e.g., municipal debt, corporate debt, and most likely stocks when the next crisis hits.

    Because inflation has rendered outright money printing politically unacceptable, policymakers will present these policies in formats that are political palatable, e.g., QE to combat climate change, debt forgiveness for students, seniors and other politically important classes, stimulus checks specifically aimed at benefitting minorities, etc. We'll delve into this more later in this chapter.

3. The monetary policies and stimulus programs introduced will have unforeseen, negative consequences.

There is no such thing as a free lunch, even for central banks or governments. Just as the policy responses to the economic shutdowns of 2020-2021 resulted in inflation, supply chain disruptions, labor issues, etc., the next round of central bank interventions will also result in unforeseen negative consequences that will cause structural damage to the economy and financial system.

4. Once these consequences become politically toxic and/or create a speculative bubble, policymakers will attempt to normalize monetary policy. And thanks to the last few business cycles we now have a checklist for ascertaining when the Fed will finally move to curtail excessive speculation:

    a. The financial system is showing clear signs of froth and/or a bubble? CHECK!

    b. The Fed is way behind the curve in terms of normalizing policy? CHECK!

    c. Everyone **knows** the Fed is way behind the curve to the point that the Fed is becoming something of a joke? CHECK!

    However, because the financial system will have become addicted to the new interventions, the normalization process will be slow or a case of too little, too late (much like the Fed's response to inflation in 2021).

5. The Fed's attempt at normalization will fail when something breaks in the financial system, bringing us back to #1 in this list, and the whole process starts over again.

The ~450 words in the above list might be the single most important words I've written in my career: this is THE framework for central banks and their policies going forward.

Japan has been cycling through this framework since **1990**. The U.S. and the rest of the world have been doing it in some form since 2003. **And since 2008, the speed and intensity of these cycle have increased dramatically.**

However, when we talk about the "speed" of a business cycle, we are talking about months if not years. Case in point, the COVID-19 cycle, which was arguably the most rapid shift from a deflationary crash to an egregiously frothy bubble in the modern era, **took 18 months.**

So don't expect the above list to play out quickly. These things take time. To show you what I mean, let's run down the last few business cycles as well as policymakers' responses to them.

A Brief, Illustrated History of Monetary Insanity

As far as monetary policy goes, historically the Fed has employed two primary tools to ease monetary conditions. They are:

1. Cutting interest rates.

2. Printing money and using it to buy assets (QE).

Regarding #1, in the U.S. since 1980, the framework has looked like the following chart.

This is a chart of the Effective Federal Funds Rate, or the "interest rate" that the Fed uses to loosen or tighten monetary policy.

Chart 9: Effective Fed Funds Rate (1980-2024)

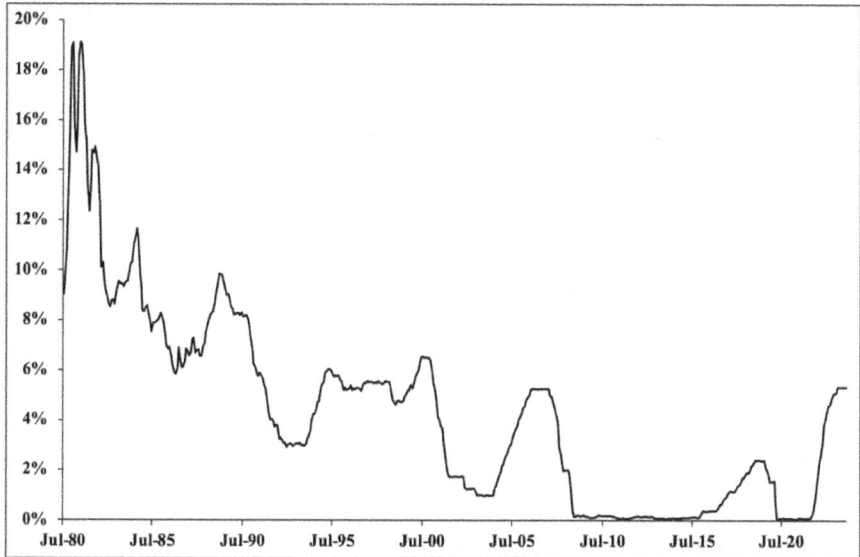

Note: Data adapted from the Federal Reserve Bank of St. Louis[8]

The first thing you'll note in the above chart is that it trended DOWN from 1982 to 2022. This means that for 40 years, each cycle saw the Fed raise rates *and* lower rates to lower levels. This is what I meant by #2 in our list above:

> *#2: Policymakers will move to deal with this problem by introducing monetary policies and stimulus programs that are more extreme than those they used to combat the previous crisis.*

In this context, the arrival of inflation has been something of a gamechanger in that it forced the Fed to raise rates significantly above their prior peak. As I write this in early 2024, the Fed Funds Rate is 5.50% compared to the previous cycle high of 2.5% in mid-2019.

The issue now is whether the Fed is indeed serious about ending inflation or not.

If the Fed *is* serious about ending inflation, then we can expect the Fed to tighten monetary conditions until a major recession hits or something systemic breaks. This would trigger a crisis or bear market in risk assets during which deflation would overwhelm any inflationary pressures in the financial system. This would mean risk assets (stocks, real estate, etc.) collapsing in value while U.S. Treasuries rally on safe haven buying.

To combat this deflationary collapse, the Fed would aggressively ease monetary conditions, cutting interest rates to zero or potentially into negative territory (both the European Central Bank and the Bank of Japan have introduced negative interest rates in the past). The Fed would also engage in even more extraordinary monetary measures to reflate the financial system (more on this later).

In this scenario, the framework that existed from 1982 to 2022 would continue: inflation would disappear from the financial system and the Fed would end up cutting rates to new lows while engaging in even greater monetary policies and stimulative efforts to combat the crisis.

By way of contrast, if the Fed *isn't* serious about ending inflation, then we can expect it to abandon its monetary tightening as soon as the U.S. enters a recession or things become seriously problematic in the financial system. As a result of this, inflation would remain in the financial system.

There is some evidence that this might prove to be the ultimate outcome for the financial system today. Thus far the Fed has proven to be *extremely* trigger happy when it comes to money printing at the first sign of trouble during this tightening cycle. Case in point, the Fed pumped $400 billion in liquidity into the financial system in just three weeks when several regional banks collapsed in March of 2023.

To put this into perspective, the Fed had only drained about $600 billion in liquidity via QT in the preceding nine months. So, the Fed effectively undid two-thirds of that in a matter of weeks. And bear in mind, the situation in March 2023 was nowhere near a full-scale crisis: peak to trough the S&P 500 only fell ~6% and actually closed out March at the month's highs!

What would our financial system look like if the Fed doesn't have what it takes to end inflation in the U.S.?

In simple terms, the U.S. would begin to resemble an emerging market with high inflation, stocks going much higher in nominal terms, bond yields that are negative in real (inflation-adjusted) terms, and a weak currency.

Remember, stocks are something of an inflation hedge. So, they would rally quite a lot if inflation were to become systemic in the U.S. However, much of this performance would be the result of the fact that stocks are priced in U.S. dollars, and the dollar would be weak due to inflation. If you've ever priced an emerging market index in its domestic currency, you'll see what I mean. The results look incredible, but you're pricing those stocks in a currency that is falling.

In terms of bonds, yields would remain high in nominal terms, but would be negative in real or inflation-adjusted terms. Perhaps the yield on the 10-Year U.S. Treasury would stay around 5% while inflation was at 6%.

A great example of this phenomenon recently played out in Argentina. In 2023, the yields on Argentina's government bonds traded between 20% and 40% in nominal terms depending on their duration (one year to 30 years). That sounds like a lot until you consider that inflation was over 100% in Argentina. So, in "real" or inflation-adjusted terms, the yield on Argentina's government bonds were *extremely* negative, (yield of 40% minus inflation of 100%= real yield of -60%).

Put simply, if the Fed abandons its goal of ending inflation, then the old framework of rates always going to new lows with each successive crisis would no longer be true. Instead, rates would remain at elevated levels (5%+), but inflation would be even higher. In this sense, rates of 5% would actually mean "easy monetary policy" or "negative real rates."

But what about money printing/QE? Would the framework of near-constant balance sheet expansion that began in 2008 continue?

Glad you asked!

Below is a chart of the Fed's balance sheet going back to 2003. You can think of this chart as illustrating how much money printing the Fed has performed over the last 20 years: the Fed's balance sheet **only grows** when the Fed prints money and uses it to buy assets.

By way of contrast, the Fed's balance sheet drops when the Fed sells assets, or allows them to mature, at which point the money the Fed spent buying the asset is returned to the U.S. Treasury.

Finally, recessions are illustrated by gray dashed rectangles in the below chart. Note that the recession during the Great Financial Crisis was about 18 months in length, while the recession triggered by the pandemic was only about three months in length.

You'll also note that with each crisis, the Fed's balance sheet has grown by greater and greater amounts. It grew a total of ~$3 trillion after the Great Financial Crisis of 2008. It later grew by ~$5 trillion following the pandemic.

Based on this, our framework suggests that whenever the next crisis hits or the economy finally enters a recession, the Fed will likely perform even *more* money printing than it did from 2020 to 2022.

I don't have a specific number in mind, but I wouldn't be surprised to see the Fed print $7 trillion or even $9 trillion to reflate the financial system after the next crisis. I realize this sounds insane now, but if you'd suggested the Fed might spend $5 trillion any time before 2020, you'd have sounded crazy, and yet that's precisely what the Fed did from 2020 to 2022.

Chart 10: Total Assets of Federal Reserve Banks, Trillions US Dollars (2006-2022)

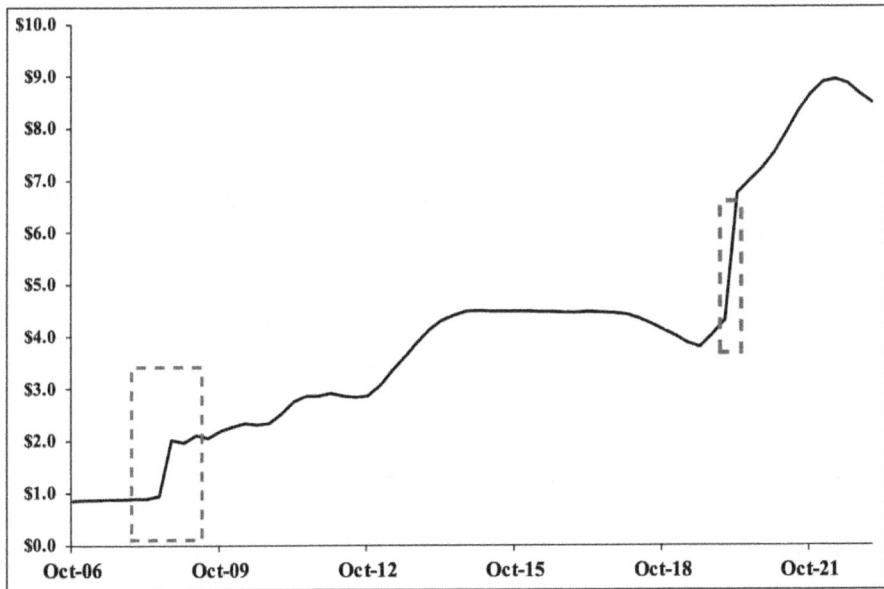

Note: Data adapted from the Federal Reserve Bank of St. Louis[2]

Remember, once a central bank embarks on a path of extraordinary monetary policy it can NEVER normalize. This was the case for the Bank of Japan starting in 1999 and it has been the case for the Fed since 2008.

In this context, regardless of whether or not the Fed is serious about tackling inflation, we can expect the Fed's balance sheet to increase by quite a lot whenever the next crisis hits.

At its peak in mid-2022, the Fed's balance sheet hit ~$9 trillion. With U.S. GDP at ~$22 trillion at that time, this meant the Fed's balance sheet was equal to roughly 40% of U.S. GDP. That seems like quite a lot until you consider that the Bank of Japan has a balance sheet that is over 130% of Japan's GDP. And while the U.S. might never get to that point, we'll likely see the Fed's balance sheet hit 60% of GDP or even 80% of GDP when the next crisis hits.

This means **a Fed balance sheet of $15+ trillion.**

But surely all this money printing would force the USD lower?

Correct. And that's the point. If a crisis hits while inflation is still deeply embedded in the financial system because the Fed has abandoned its goal of taming inflation, then the Fed will have to make a choice: either save bonds or save the USD.

Saving bonds means the U.S. avoids a debt crisis and Treasuries remain the bedrock of the financial system. Saving the USD means a debt crisis. And a debt crisis means systemic risk.

Which do you think the Fed would prefer?

So, while the Fed's approach to interest rates might change during the next crisis (meaning it no longer cuts rates to new lows), the Fed's approach to printing money will likely become even more aggressive. This brings us to #3 in our framework from the beginning of this chapter:

The monetary policies and stimulus programs introduced will have unforeseen, negative consequences.

What will the unintended consequences of future Fed monetary madness be? It's difficult to say... my best guess would be greater wealth concentration, higher inflation, and a weaker USD.

Let's dive in.

The Dark Truth About *Who* Benefits the Most from the Fed's Bubbles and Extreme Easing

As you've no doubt noticed, I'm not a fan of what the Fed has done for the last 30-odd years.

Why is this?

Well for starters, we know that printing money doesn't create significant economic growth, nor does it create jobs, nor does it boost incomes.

We explored this at length in Chapter 2. But setting aside in-depth analysis, even basic common sense tells us that money printing doesn't lead to economic success. If it did, countries like Zimbabwe and Venezuela would be economic powerhouses instead of economic basket-cases.

There is perhaps *some evidence* that printing money (QE) can stop a crisis from reaching its full potential, **but even these claims tend to be flimsy**.

Case in point, the Fed's $1 trillion QE program announced in November 2008 accomplished little if anything: stocks collapsed another 15% and the economy didn't stop contracting until seven months later.

By way of contrast, the Fed's "unlimited" QE announced in March 2020 *did* mark the bottom for the stock market, while the economy moved out of recession a mere three months later. However, since that recession was triggered by lockdowns, not an organic contraction, it's difficult to discern the effect of QE. After all, simply re-opening the economy was going to create an economic boom.

In summation: looking at the last 20 years of Fed policy, at best you can say that large-scale QE programs introduced during a crisis can *sometimes* stop a collapse from worsening.

This is hardly a track record you'd call successful. Especially when you're talking about spending TRILLIONS of dollars on these QE programs.

While QE isn't great at generating economic growth or stopping crises, it is fantastic at increasing wealth concentration and wealth inequality. Loose monetary policy *inherently* benefits the wealthy because they can leverage up (borrow money at ultra-low rates) to acquire assets and expand their wealth. To understand what I mean by this, let's use a hypothetical example.

Consider two Americans, one a billionaire, the other a middle-class individual who earns $75,000 per year and has $100,000 in a 401(k).

When the Fed creates a bubble with zero interest rate policy (ZIRP) and QE, the billionaire can take advantage of low interest rates to borrow hundreds of millions of dollars to acquire real estate, stocks and other risk assets.

With rates at 0.25%, a billionaire could borrow $100 million and only need $250,000 per year to service that loan. Meanwhile, he or she can put that $100 million to work in stocks, real estate, bonds or some other risk asset that will benefit from the Fed easing monetary policy.

During the pandemic, the S&P 500 rose 45% from 2020 to 2022. If our billionaire invested the borrowed $100 million into stocks, he or she would have generated $44.5 million in net profits ($45 million in profits minus two years' worth of debt servicing costs at $250,000 per year). That's $22.25 MILLION in new wealth per year, during a pandemic courtesy of Fed monetary policy.

Bear in mind, this calculation involves our billionaire borrowing money. The fact is that his or her pre-existing assets also would have increased in value due to the Fed's policies. Given that real estate and the stock market rose by double digit percentage gains in 2020 and 2021 during the pandemic, it wouldn't be a stretch to assume that our billionaire would see his or her net worth increase by hundreds of millions of dollars just based on what he or she already owned.

The above analysis is not just hypothetical conjecture. U.S. billionaires saw their wealth grow by $1.8 TRILLION (one thousand eight hundred billions) during the pandemic. And they weren't the only ones getting dramatically richer. Nearly 100 individuals *became* billionaires during the pandemic.

Let's compare the above outcomes to those experienced by our hypothetical middle-class person with $100,000 in a 401(k).

Assuming this person had the wherewithal to NOT sell stocks during the 2020 meltdown and then successfully rode the entire subsequent bubble, he or she would have made... $45,000 in profits. Bear in mind that's $45,000 in profits he or she couldn't touch because it was in a retirement account.

Just to make this more interesting, let's assume that our middle-class person also likes to trade the stock market outside of his or her retirement account. Let's also assume that he or she was able to time the market perfectly during the pandemic and decided to buy call options (leveraged derivatives) on stocks right around the time the Fed announced unlimited QE and stocks bottomed.

In this scenario it is possible our middle-class investor might generate several million dollars in gains. But this assumes A) that he or she somehow had the ability to time the market successfully during the first economic shutdown in American history, and B) that he or she walked away from the markets rather than continuing to trade the markets aggressively after generating his or her millions.

Perhaps just a handful of people in the entire country (330 million people) could have done this. And even then, their net worth increased by ~$1 or $2 million while our hypothetical billionaire likely saw his or her net worth increase by $100+ million over the same time period.

As I mentioned earlier, ZIRP and QE aren't great at generating economic growth or stopping crises, but they are fantastic at increasing wealth concentration and wealth inequality. The unintended consequence of this is that Fed interventions are becoming politically toxic.

The Pandemic is Over, But Uncle Sam Never Stopped Spending

The other unintended consequence of money printing concerns Uncle Sam's stimulus payments.

As I've noted previously, the Federal Government pumped some $6 trillion into the economy in the form of stimulus programs from 2020 through 2022. This hasn't stopped. As I write this in 2024, the Federal Government is running its largest peace-time deficit as a percentage of GDP: over $1.6 trillion. This means the government is spending $1.6 trillion more than it takes in via taxes every year.

Bear in mind, this is happening when the economy is *still growing*. Historically, the government runs large deficits to cushion recessions! So, we can assume that this spending will increase, not decrease when the next recession hits.

All of this is highly inflationary… and will lead to another bout of inflation (assuming inflation was wiped out in the first place) OR a worsening of inflationary conditions if inflation isn't wiped out when the next recession hits.

Why?

Because stimulus increases demand above what would be normal during a contraction. We saw this during the shutdowns. And with emergency levels of government spending now normalized (again, the Biden Administration is running emergency levels of spending at a time when the economy is still growing), we can safely assume this will not change during the next recession.

This is also politically toxic. Economists tell us that inflation has rapidly declined, but a recent *CBS poll* from December 2023 showed that Americans' standard of living is worse, not better, than their parents' was. All told, 76% of Americans state that their incomes are not keeping up with inflation.

This brings us to #4 and #5 in our list from the beginning of this chapter:

3. Once the unforeseen consequences of stimulus/ monetary easing become politically toxic, policymakers will attempt to normalize monetary policies and stimulus programs. However, because the financial system has become addicted to said programs, the normalization process will be slow and likely a case of too little, too late.

4. The attempt at normalization will fail when something breaks in the financial system, and we return to #1.

We are now talking about things that will unfold months if not years from the time of this writing. It's extremely difficult to predict the future more than three to six months out, particularly in terms of macro developments.

However, history has been very clear as far as inflation goes. Once a country experiences a major bout of inflation, traditional money printing becomes politically toxic. So even if this future crisis occurs five or 10 years from now, the memory of this current bout of inflation will still be quite fresh. Ask anyone who lived through the 1970s about what it was like, and they'll tell you it was horrific... and that was 50 years ago!

For this reason, whenever the Fed is eventually forced to ease monetary conditions again in the future, it will need to do so in manner that is as **politically benign** as possible. In this context, I believe we will see two types of monetary policy introduced by the Fed during its next easing cycle.

They are:

1. More "politically acceptable" versions of current Fed policies, e.g., Yield Curve Control and buying stocks outright.

2. Completely new, unorthodox monetary policies aimed specifically at political issues that are completely outside the scope of the Fed's Dual Mandate, e.g., programs designed to combat climate change, racial disparities in income/wealth, etc.

Put simply, the Fed is going to get **politically correct**.

Yield Curve Control: QE With a Purpose!

The easiest means for the Fed to ease monetary conditions at a time when money printing is politically toxic is to shift its QE programs from being "open-ended" to being "context specific."

Japan's central bank, called the Bank of Japan (BoJ), employed this exact strategy via a program called "yield curve control" in 2016.

At that time, the BoJ had just discovered that the gigantic "shock and awe" QE program it introduced in 2014 (a single QE program equal to 25% of Japan's GDP), had failed to generate any sustainable economic growth. So, the BoJ was looking for a new way to employ QE that didn't sound like the same old same old.

They turned to yield curve control (YCC).

In its simplest rendering, the BoJ stated that any time the yield on the 10-year Japanese Government Bond rose above 0%, the BoJ would print money and use it to buy those bonds, thereby forcing their yields back down.

On the surface, this sounded much more palatable to voters. After all, the central bank was now printing money and buying assets ONLY when it was warranted, instead of printing a fixed amount of money every month and using it to buy assets regardless of market conditions.

However, this is something of a ruse.

Yield curve control is still QE, it's just presented as being focused on a particular goal (keeping yields low). And since the average voter doesn't fully understand what QE is to begin with, this is a lot more acceptable, than "the Fed is printing $120 billion per month!"

Of course, the dirty secret about yield curve control is that it is in fact an **open-ended** program that runs ad infinitum or until something "breaks" in the system. Indeed, yield curve control could potentially involve printing even MORE money than your typical fixed QE program. After all, what happens if yields keep rising? The central bank will be forced to keep printing more money!

So, you can see why central banks love this idea. It gives them the means to print money ad infinitum, without triggering outrage in the general population. Moreover, yield curve control signals to the bond market that a central bank is willing to buy "unlimited amounts" of certain bonds at certain prices. This is the equivalent of the central bank drawing a line in the sand and telling the market, *"I'll shoot you with a bazooka if you cross this."*

Now, I know some of you are no doubt saying to yourselves, *"That's great, Graham, but Japan is not the U.S. There is no way the Fed could get away with something like this."*

Think again.

The Fed employed yield curve control during the latter half of the 1940s. Prior to that, the U.S. government had been running massive deficits to finance its war efforts during WWII. With the war now over, the bond markets had become concerned that the U.S. was overly indebted and would have trouble returning to normal fiscal policy.

To combat this, the Fed announced YCC for most major Treasury durations (short-term, medium-term, and long-term Treasury bonds). Treasury investors weren't too happy with this, so they started dumping Treasuries. The Fed was then forced to acquire ALL the Treasury bonds that investors dumped!

This meant a **10-FOLD increase** in the Fed's account from 1941 to 1945. And if you think that sounds crazy, consider that during this period, **the Fed ended up owning 75% of all outstanding short-term Treasuries.**

Yes, you read that correctly, 75%. And as crazy as it sounds, the policy worked (yields came down). However, breaking free of these policies was not easy: it took the Fed a full decade to normalize from YCC.

I fully expect the Fed to introduce YCC at some point in the not-so-distant future. Whether the Fed will end up owning 75% of the T-bill market, I have no idea. The BoJ has managed to acquire over 50% of all Japanese Bonds during the last 30 years. If the Fed were to follow a similar trajectory, it would end up owning over $16 trillion worth of Treasuries. I realize that sounds insane, but the Fed currently owns over $5 trillion worth of Treasuries. That would have sounded insane back in 2008 and yet, here we are!

So, we can expect the Fed to introduce YCC whenever the next crisis hits. But that's not the only politically palatable intervention the Fed will introduce... I also expect the Fed will begin buying stocks and stock-based ETFs.

The Fed Will *Officially* Become a Stock Investor

As I noted in Chapter 1, when the Fed began buying corporate debt, corporate debt ETFs, auto loans, and other assets in 2020, it was *technically* breaking the law; the Federal Reserve Act of 1913 explicitly forbids the Fed from buying these assets.

The Fed got around this issue by using U.S. Treasury credit facilities to facilitate the actual purchases; the Fed printed money and gave the money to the Treasury, which then used the money to buy the assets. And the Fed used this scheme to buy every asset you can think of except commodities (oil, gold, etc.).

Specifically, the Fed bought:

1. U.S. Treasuries.

2. Mortgage-Backed Securities.

3. Corporate debt from individual companies like Apple, Toyota, etc.

4. Corporate debt that was packed into funds called Exchange Traded Funds (ETFs) which trade like stocks.

5. Municipal debt issued by cities, states, and municipalities.

6. Bundles of Certificates of Deposit.

7. Bundles of Student Loans.

8. Bundles of Auto Loans.

9. Money market funds.

10. Commercial paper (short-term corporate debt that companies use to make payroll and other short-term needs).

Having established this kind of precedent in 2020, I fully expect that the Fed will use a similar scheme to start buying stock ETFs as well as individual stocks when the next crisis hits.

After all, the Fed has already bought assets that trade on the stock market (corporate bond ETFs). So, the jump to buying stock-based ETFs or individual stocks isn't even that large of a leap!

If you think this sounds impossible, think again. Globally, central banks have been buying stocks for decades. The Swiss National Bank (SNB) buys individual stocks all the time to the tune of billions of dollars (~$150 billion in total at the time of this writing).

However, even those purchases pale in comparison to what the Bank of Japan has done.

For 11 years from 2010 until 2021, the BoJ routinely bought stock-based ETFs via multiple QE programs. And we're not talking about a few thousand yens worth here and there. As I mentioned in Chapter 2, the BoJ has spent so much money buying stocks that it:

1. Is the single largest holder of Japanese stocks in the world.

2. Owns 7% of the entire Japanese stock market.

3. Is a top 10 shareholder for over half the companies that trade on the Nikkei.

So not only is there a precedent for central banks to buy stocks, but this policy has actually been taken to the *extreme* in the case of the BoJ. Moreover, it's important to note that no central bankers associated with these policies were fired or forced to resign in disgrace.

I fully believe that just as the Fed has followed the BoJ's lead on Zero Interest Rate Policy (ZIRP), Quantitative Easing (QE) and other policies, it will also start buying stocks outright, albeit to a lesser degree when the next crisis hits.

And unlike traditional QE which has been described as "bailing out Wall Street," the Fed will have plenty of political cover to justify buying stocks.

Why Stock-Based QE is More Politically Palatable Than Anything the Fed Has Done Previously

First and foremost, we have to remember that the Fed has already bought Treasuries, corporate debt, municipal debt, and slew of other assets during the 2020 crash without much public outcry. Few if any Americans own those asset classes. If anything, the Fed was bailing out corporations and municipalities when it bought them.

By way of contrast, more than HALF of all American households (~55%) have exposure to the stock market. Indeed, stocks are arguably the single most-owned asset class in the United States with the exception of real estate (homeownership is ~60%).

The Fed could easily argue that buying stocks or stock-based ETFs would *help* Main Street America since it would mean boosting the net worth of more than half of American households. The Fed could even frame a stock-based QE program as "bailing out Main Street."

If you think this sounds insane, policymakers actually bought stocks before, though few people knew about it: during the depths of the 2008 crisis, when everyone was too worried about the collapse of the financial system to complain, **the Treasury bought $20 billion worth of Bank of America and Citigroup's stock.**

Granted, this was the Treasury, not the Federal Reserve, but my point is that there is some precedent for policymakers to buy stocks directly during crises. And given that the Fed was able to buy multiple asset classes outside the scope of its normal operations during the 2020 crash, it's highly likely that during the next crisis, the Fed will do the same thing, only for stocks.

When it does, the Fed will use a similar scheme to that which it employed during the pandemic: the Fed will print money, transfer it to the credit facility run by the U.S. Treasury, and the Treasury will buy the stocks.

In terms of size, the Fed's first QE program announced in 2008 involved the purchase of $600 billion worth of Mortgage-Backed Securities (MBS). I suspect the Fed's first stock-based QE program would be introduced in a similar manner: e.g. a $500 billion program introduced as an emergency measure during a crisis or market crash.

However, regardless of its size, I expect the Fed would rapidly normalize this policy. After all, that's been the case for the BoJ for more than two decades. And as we've seen time and again, the Fed has been running the BoJ's playbook since 2008.

The BoJ first started buying stock-based exchange traded funds (ETFs) in October 2010. At that time, the policy was introduced as an emergency measure: the program was supposed to last 14 months and consist of 450 billion yens worth of purchases.

Four months after it was introduced, the BoJ expanded the plan to 900 billion yen and extended the program's deadline to June 2012. In August 2011, the BoJ expanded the program to 1.4 trillion yen and extended its deadline to the end of 2012.

This QE program briefly ended then, only to be re-opened as an open-ended (meaning no deadline at all) program that would involve 1 trillion yens worth of purchases **every single year** starting in April 2013. And when that didn't prove adequate to meet the BoJ's goals, in July 2016 the BoJ increased the pace of its annual ETF-based QE program to SIX TRILLION YEN.

This amounted to ~1% of the Nikkei's market cap at the time.

So, in the span of six years, Japan's experiment with stock-based QE went from being a temporary, emergency program of 450 billion yen to a permanent, open-ended program equal to 1% of the total stock market per year.

More importantly from the perspective of career-focused central bankers, no policymaker was fired for this insanity. In fact, the central banker who oversaw the BoJ's foray into stock-buying, Haruhiko Kuroda, remained in charge of the BoJ through 2023 when he retired not because of the insanity of his monetary policies, but because his term had ended, and he was *tired of running the BoJ.*

I expect that the Fed's foray into stock-based QE will follow a similar pattern, first introduced as a temporary emergency measure that will rapidly be normalized. And I also expect that the Fed will eventually become the single largest holder of U.S. stocks in the world.

I realize that last statement is quite dramatic. But this is what happened for every other asset class the Fed has bought via prior large-scale QE programs.

Remember, when the Fed first introduced QE, it was supposed to be an *emergency* program designed to stop the Great Financial Crisis in 2008. Since that time, the Fed has run QE in one form or another during 9 of the last 14 years, spending a total of $8 TRILLION. Today, the Fed is now the largest owner of both U.S. Treasuries ($5.7 trillion) and Mortgage-Backed Securities ($2.7 trillion) in the world.

With that in mind, I wouldn't be surprised if the Fed buys over $3 trillion worth of stocks in the next decade.

For those critics who will argue that the Fed buying stocks isn't politically acceptable due to it benefiting the 1% or increasing wealth inequality, I believe that whenever the Fed begins buying stocks outright via the Treasury, the federal government would also introduce multiple programs designed to help more Americans own stocks.

One such scheme would be the normalization of fractional shares in stocks, meaning you buy a fraction of a single share, say ¼ or ½ of a share instead of a total share.

What would this accomplish?

The share prices for high-quality businesses (Apple, Amazon, Exxon, etc.) typically cost tens, if not hundreds of dollars. By way of contrast, those companies with low share prices (a few dollars or even just pennies) are usually of extremely low quality.

Fractional shares would allow an investor to own a piece of Apple or Amazon for just $10 or even less. This practice already exists for some brokers (Robinhood, Interactive Brokers, Charles Schwab), **but I expect it to become the industry standard in the coming months and years.**

The normalization of fractional shares would allow every American, even those in the lower wealth percentiles, to have some stock exposure. Sure, this idea is fraught with risk (stocks are volatile assets), but when has that stopped the government from doing anything?

Case in point, the entire Housing Bubble of 2003-2008 was the result of the Federal Government pushing to increase homeownership in the U.S., and none of the politicians or policymakers who pushed for that were kicked out of office when the whole mess came crashing down in 2008.

Speaking of which, when the next crisis hits, I also expect the Fed to expand its QE program for Mortgage-Backed Securities (MBS) aggressively. Why? For the exact same reason that the Fed will begin buying stocks: because real estate is an asset class that is closely aligned with Americans' wealth.

Moreover, as the Fed discovered in 2020, going "big" with MBS purchases can force the real estate market to reflate rapidly. Given that the Fed was buying everything under the sun at that time, and everyone was terrified about potentially dying from covid, the details of this were easy to miss. So, let's run a quick review.

How the Fed Cornered the MBS Market… and Created a Housing Bubble in Six Months Flat

The MBS market, like everything else, began to break down in March 2020 due to the shutdowns. So, on March 15th, the Fed announced it intended to spend $200 billion buying MBS securities.

The Fed spent $67 billion of that money in the first seven days of the program.

To put this into perspective, prior to this, the Fed's largest MBS QE program had been $60 billion **per month**. So, when the Fed found that buying $67 billion worth of MBS in a single week wasn't adequate to calm the markets, **it announced it would buy up to $50 billion in MBS *per day.***

The message was clear: the Fed intended to corner the MBS market. And that's just what it did.

The Fed spent $183 BILLION buying MBS in the week of March 23rd. And it continued buying MBS hand over fist for the next three months. Indeed, the Fed was still buying MBS at a pace of $22 billion *per week* through the months of May and June 2020.

The end result? Take a look at what happened to the median price of U.S. homes once the Fed began cornering the MBS market.

Chart 11: Median Sales Price of Houses Sold For United States, Thousands US Dollars (2017-2022)

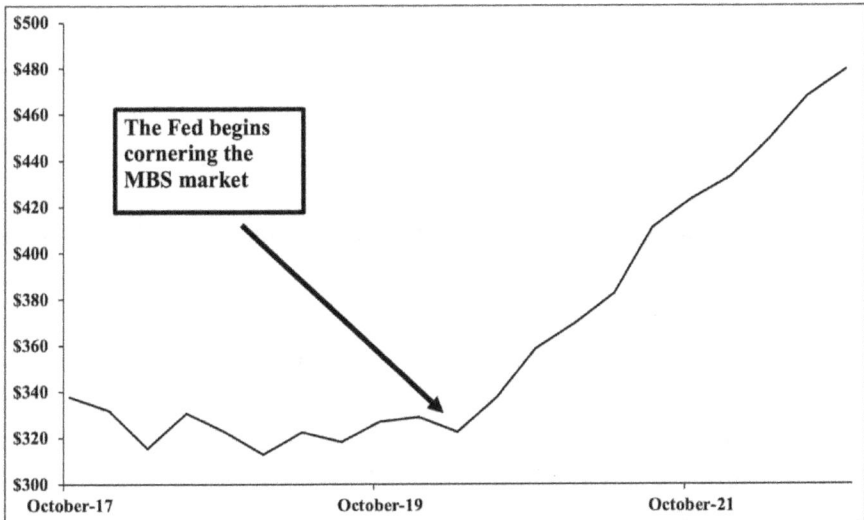

Note: Data adapted from U.S. Census Bureau and U.S. Department of Housing and Urban Development[9]

Yes, you're seeing that correctly, the median home price in the U.S. rose by 33% in the span of two years after the Fed cornered the MBS market. Historically, real estate appreciates at a pace of 1%-2% per year. **But within six months of the Fed cornering the MBS market, home prices were appreciating at a pace of over 10% per year!**

The Fed learned an important lesson here: cut rates to zero and give the MBS market a buyer with bottomless pockets so mortgage companies can unload their loans in the secondary market and BOOM you get a housing bubble.

With that in mind, whenever the next crisis hits, I expect the Fed will employ this same strategy again. After all, real estate is the single most-owned asset class and represents the single largest purchase of most Americans' lifetimes. In this context, the Fed's QE programs for buying

MBS represents one of the most direct means of boosting Americans' household wealth.

Moreover, now that the Fed has figured out that it can stop a real estate crisis on a dime and then reflate a housing bubble in just six months, what are the odds Fed officials will suddenly become humble about this monetary power?

Having said that, most Americans don't know what an MBS is, nor do they care. So, when the Fed starts cornering this market again, I suspect it will frame the policy in politically acceptable terms, e.g. "boosting the housing market" or "rebuilding household wealth."

We've covered a lot of ground here, so let's run a quick review of the new policies I expect the Fed to introduce when the next crisis arrives:

1. Yield curve control, or the policy of buying Treasuries of certain duration any time their yields rise above a target level.

2. Stock-based QE.

3. Large-scale MBS-based QE programs.

The above policies, while outrageous, are really just a "rebranding" of what the Fed has already done: YCC is QE on demand with a particular goal in mind, while the Fed buying stocks and MBS represent the Fed shifting the focus of its QE programs from assets that are primarily owned by Wall Street (corporate bonds, Treasuries, etc.) to assets that are primarily owned by Main Street (stocks and residential real estate).

In this sense, these policies are more politically palatable than the traditional QE programs the Fed used to buy Treasuries. Instead of "bailing out Wall Street" or giving "handouts to the rich," the Fed could argue that it is simply trying to "keep interest rates low to make housing more affordable" or is "buying stocks to boost household net worth for the majority of Americans."

Moreover, the above policies are in fact the future monetary policies I anticipate the Fed will introduce when the next crisis hits. I believe that the Fed will also introduce new, completely unorthodox monetary policies that are specifically aimed at political issues outside the scope of the Fed's Dual Mandate, e.g., programs designed to combat climate change, racial disparities in income/wealth, etc.

The reason?

The Fed Is Now a Political Entity

Historically, the Fed has been viewed as a politically *independent* entity.

For example, Fed Chairs, who are nominated by the President of the United States, are often from opposing political parties. A good example of this is Ben Bernanke, a Republican, who was reappointed Fed Chair by President Barack Obama, a Democrat.

Of course, the choosing of a Fed chair from an opposing political party is mostly symbolic, just as the Fed's political independence is something of a fairy tale. No major entity in the D.C. area is apolitical or immune to political pressure. This is particularly true for the Fed, which exerts tremendous influence on both the stock market and the economy: two items with massive political implications.

Moreover, there is plenty of evidence to suggest the Fed has engaged in politically motivated policies in the past. A great example is when the Bernanke-led Fed decided to launch QE 3 just two months before the 2012 Presidential election, thereby boosting the economy and stock market to aid President Obama's re-election bid.

Another example concerns when the Powell-led Fed raised rates a fourth time in 2018 thereby cratering the stock market: a move that former Fed Vice-Chair Stanley Fisher later admitted in an interview was an attempt to hinder the Trump administration's economic goals.

However, up until recently, the Fed's political inclinations were more implicit than explicit in nature. What I mean by this is that while the Fed may have engaged in policies that were driven at least in part by politics, those political elements were never stated publicly. And they certainty weren't presented as the primary focus of the Fed's activities.

Not anymore.

Between 2020 and 2022, Fed leadership became increasingly vocal about politics, particularly progressive social-justice issues. Historically, speeches by Fed leadership focused on things like "interest rates" "employment" and "growth." But starting in mid-2020, Fed speakers started addressing issues such as "climate change," "racism," "diversity" and the like.

Below is a list of some of the more astonishing statements made by Fed Chair Jerome Powell (emphasis added).

> *"Finally, I want to acknowledge the tragic events that have again put a **spotlight on the pain of racial injustice** in this country...The Federal Reserve serves the entire nation. We operate in, and are part of, many of the communities across the country where Americans are grappling with and expressing themselves on issues of racial equality."* (Fed FOMC Q&A Session, June 2020).

> *"**What we're really working on is: how do we incorporate climate change risk into all that we do...** It has potential implications for monetary policy, for bank regulation, for financial stability, and I would say we're in the very early stages of trying to work through what that means for our goals."* (European Central Bank Panel, November 2020)

*"**There is no doubt that climate change poses profound challenges** for the global economy and certainly the financial system." (Green Swan Conference, June 2021).*

*"Throughout my career, in both the public and the private sectors, I have seen that the best and most successful organizations are often the ones that have a **strong and persistent commitment to diversity and inclusion**...These organizations consistently attract the best talent, by investing in and retaining a world-class workforce." (Conference on Diversity and Inclusion, November 2021)*

On a personal or private basis, a Fed official can talk about whatever he or she likes; they are individuals with their own opinions. However, when a Fed official makes a public statement as a representative of the central bank, that's a whole different matter. And NOWHERE in the Fed's official mandates as established by the Federal Reserve Act of 1913 nor in its amendment in 1977, are there references to ANY of this stuff.

By quick way of review, the Fed's Dual Mandate is:

"to maintain long-run growth of the monetary and credit aggregates commensurate with the economy's long-run potential to increase production, so as to promote effectively the goals of maximum employment, stable prices and moderate long-term interest rates."

You could *technically* argue that maximum employment involves issues of racial inequality as far as employment is concerned, but that is a stretch. Issues like climate change and racial injustice, however, have absolutely NOTHING to do with the Fed's responsibilities.

If you think I'm being too critical here, imagine if Department of Justice officials started talking about issues that are primarily the domain of the Fed, e.g. the Attorney General of the United States held a press conference to address the urgent issue of "the exchange rate of the U.S. dollar to the Yen" and you'll see what I mean.

I'm not saying that racial justice or climate change are not issues; I'm saying that the U.S. central bank has no business discussing them! By law, the Fed has one job: to use interest rates to ensure economic growth with minimal inflation… and they haven't even been able to do that successfully, as the last 100+ years have illustrated.

So why is the Fed suddenly spouting off on all this social justice stuff? Did the individuals who sit on the Board of Governors of the Federal Reserve System all decide, by pure coincidence, that there are more important things than economics and it's time to become social justice activists?

Part of it is political pressure (everyone in the beltway is pressured to "toe the line" in terms of political narratives). However, I believe a much larger part of the Fed's sudden shift to political posturing is due to what I've been writing about for much of this chapter: that the Fed's policies have created wealth inequality and inflation to the point that said policies and the Fed itself have become politically toxic.

As a result of this, the Fed is desperate to find politically acceptable reasons to print money in the future. And progressive politics, with its emphasis on social spending, provides the perfect cover.

It's pretty clever, albeit deceitful, if you think about it. The Fed's money printing caused jaw-dropping wealth inequality, so now the Fed can pivot to claim that targeted money printing to benefit those left behind will solve this!

For those who don't think this is possible, consider that the Fed has been bailing out/ propping up the well-connected elite for decades. And we're not talking about a small amount of money.

J.P. Morgan received $30 billion from the Fed to buy Bear Stearns in March of 2008.

That bank and five others (Goldman Sachs, Bank of America, Wells Fargo, Morgan Stanley, and Citigroup) were allowed to borrow ~$500 billion *daily* during the depths of the Great Financial Crisis.

Moreover, the Fed is not the only entity that has been handing out hundreds of billions of dollars to the well-connected elite; Uncle Sam has been doing the same thing for decades. Indeed, one could argue that most of the "pork" smuggled into new bills of legislation does precisely this.

Heck, even the Paycheck Protection Program (PPP) which was designed to help small businesses mostly went to large businesses that didn't necessarily need it: of the $500+ billion doled out in 2020, **over 70% of it went to the top 20% of the U.S. in terms of income earners.**

In this context, the Fed's sudden shift towards politically correct narratives represents policymakers asking, *"Why shouldn't the Fed intervene to help those in the lowest income brackets or those who make less for racial reasons?"*

I honestly don't have a good answer for this. Sure, you could argue that the Fed *shouldn't* have been bailing out Wall Street, which I've done for most of my career. But the fact is that the Fed *did* bail them out... so why shouldn't it bail out or help those who are less fortunate or less politically connected?

Understand, I'm not being facetious here. I really don't have a good answer for this aside from the typical, *"that's not how capitalism is supposed to work"* argument, which has been null and void for decades.

Ethics aside, the fact is that Fed leadership has begun pushing for the Fed to get involved in political hot topics that were previously outside the scope of its Dual Mandate. In light of all of this, I fully expect the

Fed to begin implementing new politically progressive forms of money printing in the coming months. This will include:

1. Money printing to benefit minorities and minority-owned small businesses.

2. Money printing to "fight" climate change.

3. Money printing to address sexism.

And more.

Welcome to the future of monetary policy: money printing with a politically correct motivation.

Politically Correct Money Printing

The key development here is the Fed shifting away from focusing on banks and hedge funds to focusing on individuals and small businesses. And this shift, however small, will eventually pave the way for Universal Income and other similar schemes through which the Fed simply prints money and passes it out to the American people.

All of it sounds crazy, but everything the Fed did in 2008 or 2020 would have sounded crazy five years prior. And the reality is that the policies I've described in this chapter are really the same old money printing, just dressed up as something new.

As such, they integrate into the monetary policy framework I laid out at the start of the chapter. If you take home one single thing from this portion of this book, it should be that framework.

By way of review, that framework is as follows:

1. Something will "break" in the financial system and/or the economy will enter a recession. Either or both developments will trigger deflation in risk assets (stocks, real estate, etc.) that will become headline news.

   That last point is key; there are ALWAYS problems in the economy and the financial markets. However, for something to warrant a major policy response, it needs to enter the public's consciousness. At that point, we proceed to #2.

2. Policymakers will deal with this problem by introducing monetary policies and stimulus programs that are more extreme than those they used to combat the previous crisis.

   These responses will break into two categories.

   a. More extreme versions of previously used policies (deeper interest rate cuts, larger QE programs).

   b. Policies that are unprecedented: buying assets that are technically outside the Fed's mandate, e.g., municipal debt, corporate debt, and most likely stocks, when the next crisis hits.

   Because inflation has rendered outright money printing politically unacceptable, policymakers will present these policies in formats that are political palatable, e.g., QE to combat climate change, debt forgiveness for students, seniors and other politically important classes, stimulus checks specifically aimed at benefitting minorities, etc.

3. The monetary policies and stimulus programs introduced will have unforeseen, negative consequences.

    There is no such thing as a free lunch, even for central banks or governments. Just as the policy responses to the economic shutdowns of 2020-2021 resulted in inflation, supply chain disruptions, labor issues, etc., the next round of central bank interventions will also result in unforeseen negative consequences that will cause structural damage to the economy and financial system.

4. Once these consequences become politically toxic and/or create a speculative bubble, policymakers will attempt to normalize monetary policy. And thanks to the last few business cycles we now have a checklist for ascertaining when the Fed will finally move to curtail excessive speculation:

    a. The financial system is showing clear signs of froth and/or a bubble? CHECK!

    b. The Fed is way behind the curve in terms of normalizing policy? CHECK!

    c. Everyone **knows** the Fed is way behind the curve to the point that the Fed is becoming something of a joke? CHECK!

However, because the financial system will have become addicted to the new interventions, the normalization process will be slow or a case of too little, too late (much like the Fed's response to inflation in 2021).

5. The Fed's attempt at normalization will fail when something breaks in the financial system, bringing us back to #1 in this list, and the whole process starts over again.

This is how things have played out for the last 50 years. It's also how they will likely play out for the foreseeable future. As such this is the roadmap for how to navigate the Fed and its future policies going forward.

This concludes this section of *Into The Abyss*. The next section will focus on how to invest in light of the material I've presented in this analysis.

PART 2:

How to Invest After the Bubble

Introduction

The remainder of this book is devoted to providing some guidelines for investing in the current central bank-controlled markets. I must warn you in advance, I won't be presenting you with "get rich quick" schemes or gimmicks.

For one thing, **none of those things work.**

Investing is a lot like fitness… there are no shortcuts. If you want to look great, you need to put in the work by eating clean and working out. And not for a short time period… but for months on end.

The people who claim they can teach you how to make millions of dollars from the markets with a course or book are no different from the people who claim they obtained "seven-minute abs" or achieved 5% body fat with "one easy trick."

I realize this flies in the face of the vast majority of investment research marketing. So, let's start this portion of the book with the Three Dirty Little Secrets of Investing.

Dirty Little Secret of Investing #1: It is IMPOSSIBLE to Get Rich *Quick* From Investing

Let's attack this from a commonsense perspective first.

If someone knew how to generate millions of dollars *quickly* from investing, why would he or she sell you that information for the price of a book or a coaching seminar? What does that say about the true value of the information? Wouldn't you expect it to cost tens if not hundreds of thousands of dollars (again, the information supposedly shows you how to make millions *quickly*)?

Secondly, anyone who *actually* **got rich quickly** from the markets did so by:

1. Getting lucky.

2. Using other people's money.

3. Both.

Nothing is free in life, especially investment gains. Any time you make a trade or an investment, you are taking on risk. And if you are looking to make a LOT of money FAST, **you will need to take on HUGE amounts of risk to do so.**

To be totally clear, occasionally there are situations in which you can potentially see a truly enormous return on your capital with minimal risk… but those are **extremely rare**. For most individual investors those situations are akin to finding a three-karat diamond while fishing in a lake: it is a once in a lifetime event… if it even happens once.

I realize this is difficult to swallow. The marketing world is awash with incredible claims of making astonishing riches from the markets. However, simple math proves that my arguments are correct.

Let's say you have $100,000 available to trade and you want to turn it into $1 million quickly. Any investment that has the potential to rise 10-fold in a short period of time (think weeks or months) **is also volatile enough to lose 99% in a short time period.**

Remember, volatility works both ways. If you want the necessary volatility to produce a 10-fold increase in value quickly, you must also stomach that same volatility to the *downside.*

Out of 100 traders who invest in an asset that is that volatile, at least 98, if not ALL of them would lose money… and not just a little, but MOST of their money. Moreover, the one or two people who did end up turning $100,000 into $1 million simply got lucky; their gains were NOT the result of some extraordinary skill. And I guarantee that the next time they take on that much risk **they'll lose most if not ALL of their money**.

The only exception to this would be the person who is capable of getting lucky the one time, who then walks away from trading forever. In 20+ years as an investment strategist I have yet to meet anyone who had that ability. Everyone I've ever met who made a lot of money quickly from the markets continued to try their luck and ended up losing most if not all of their gains.

Again, if you are looking to get rich *quick* from the markets… you are almost guaranteed to lose most, if not ALL of your money.

Having said that, you can make a LOT of money from the markets, but it takes a LOT of time and a LOT of effort to do so. When I say, "a lot of time," I mean YEARS, if not decades. If you don't believe me, let's consider the track record of the GREATEST money manager of the last 50 years.

The Greatest Money Manager Alive Today Averages 2.5% Per Month

Stanley Druckenmiller is arguably the greatest money manager of the last 50 years. For 40+ years he didn't have a single losing year. And for 30 years straight, he saw average annual gains of 30%. To put this into perspective, $1,000 invested at the start of that streak would be worth $2.6 MILLION by the end.

Again, Mr. Druckenmiller is arguably the greatest money manager of the last half century. He is the Usain Bolt or Wayne Gretsky of investing. And he returned 30% per year on average.

Notice I say, *per year...* not per week or per month.

To put this into perspective: a 30% return averaged out over a year comes to 2.5% per month.

Yes, 2.5%.

Those guys on Twitter or Facebook who claim they turned $10,000 into $5 million in a matter of months are all lying to you. The greatest money manager alive today averages **2.5% per month**.

Moreover, I should add that Druckenmiller's returns are NOT consistent. By his own admission, many of his "up years" saw gains of just 5% or 10%. It was because of the occasional outstanding year when he was up 80% or more that his returns averaged out to 30% per year.

So again, the greatest money manager of the last 50 years averaged 30% per year... and those returns were NOT consistent. Many years his returns were WAY below 30%.

Which brings us to our second Dirty Little Secret of Investing...

Dirty Little Secret of Investing #2: If You Want to Succeed As An Investor, You WILL Lose Money

Investing involves losing money. Full stop.

If you don't want to lose money, DO NOT invest your money, put it into a Certificate of Deposit or Money Market Fund instead. Investing with the expectation of not losing money is like taking up boxing with the expectation that you won't get punched in the face.

Every investor loses money. No one has a success rate of 100%. The most accurate traders in the world only make money 60% of the time. And many of the investing legends make money an even smaller percentage of the time.

Put another way, the BEST investors in the world lose money on four out of every 10 trades they made. Some make money on even fewer occasions. The difference between the folks who become legends and those traders who go broke is that the legends make a LOT of money when they are right... and lose relatively little when they are wrong.

So again, if you want to succeed at investing, you're going to have to get used to losing money on a regular basis. Moreover, the more successful you become at investing, the more money (in dollar terms) you will lose. The investing legends you hear about have ALL lost tens if not hundreds of millions if not BILLIONs of dollars in the course of their careers.

Let's consider Warren Buffett, who is arguably the most famous investor of all time. Buffett has made hundreds of investments in his career. **However, the vast bulk of his wealth was generated by just a dozen or so stocks.**

Put another way, MOST of the investments made by Warren Buffett either lost money or never amounted to much in terms of his overall wealth. The key was that he typically cut his losses relatively quickly... and made so much money from his big winners that he became extraordinarily wealthy in the process.

Moreover, it's not as if Buffett's success came easily. He had down years like everyone else. And in point of fact, MOST of his success was the product of longevity. Warren Buffett began investing at age 11. He started managing outside money at age 25. He didn't become a billionaire until age 56.

However, **he made another $111 billion from age 56 to 92.**

Note here again, one of the primary elements of Buffett's success was that he became wealthy *over time.* Buffett didn't become insanely wealthy in a matter of months or even years. It took him *decades* to become uber-rich.

Well, that and playing with Other People's Money (OPM).

Which brings us to #3 in the above list...

Dirty Little Secret of Investing #3: The Investing Legends Got Rich Using Other People's Money

Most of the famous investors you hear about became insanely wealthy because someone or "several someones" wrote them large checks to play with.

While there are some truly extraordinary investors (people who have generated fortunes solely from their trading skills), the reality is that over 98% of the "gurus" or "legends" you hear about accrued **MOST** of their wealth using OPM.

Put another way, if they were forced to trade with ONLY their own money, **they NEVER would have become super wealthy or famous.** I realize this sounds quite cynical, but it's true. MOST if not all of the hedge fund managers and investing legends you hear on TV made MOST if not ALL of their money from fees. And the larger their asset base (the money they manage) the greater the amount of money collected via fees.

Let's dive in.

First and foremost, hedge funds typically charge 2% of a client's assets up front when a client joins the fund. So, the fund manager gets paid *no matter what happens.* Even if everything goes wrong and the manager loses the clients' money, he or she keeps that initial 2% of assets. So, if he or she raises $1 billion in capital for the fund, he or she will pocket $20 million even if the fund is a disaster and ends up closing.

On top of this, hedge fund managers and many investing legends *also* take 20% of the profits they generate in their fund. And I'm not talking about 20% of the profits from their own money, **I mean 20% of the profits from the ENTIRE FUND.**

Let's say you're a hedge fund manager who manages $1 billion. Now let's say you have a great year that returns 20% or $200 million. **You get to keep 20% of that, or $40 million.**

Yes, we're talking about a $40 million payday for a single year of generating 20% from the markets. And that's EVEN if stocks rose 20% that year, meaning our hedge fund manager didn't even beat the market! Heck, he or she would keep that money even if the market as a whole rose 30% and he or she *under*-performed by 10%!

Throw in the initial 2% or $20 million the hedge fund manager made from charging his or her clients 2% when they joined the fund, and you're talking about $60 million in income from a single year of managing a fund EVEN if that 20% return trailed the market!

THAT's how most of these guys and gals get filthy rich: they make tens, if not hundreds of millions of dollars in a single year playing with other people's money, even if they don't beat the market. **All they need to do is turn a profit.**

What's even crazier is that in many cases these individuals remain rich even if they subsequently blow up and lose billions of dollars' worth of their clients' money.

Why?

Because even if they have a terrible year, wipe out 40% of their portfolio, and are forced to close shop, **they still keep 2% of the assets as well as 20% of the profits they generated prior to the bad year.**

Talk about a "heads I win, tails I DON'T lose" situation!

This is the unspoken secret about the investing world: that less than 0.1% of the so-called investing legends would be anywhere near as rich as they are if they had been forced to play ONLY with their own money.

Don't get me wrong. I'm not saying these folks *aren't* talented. It takes talent to turn a profit in the market, especially if you're able to do so for years on end. What I *am* saying is that the *bulk* of these peoples' money came from taking **HUGE bets with other people's money.**

Take Ray Dalio for instance.

Mr. Dalio has averaged 11.5% per year for the last 28 years with his Bridgewater hedge fund. **That is roughly double the S&P 500's performance and is truly incredible!**

However, had Mr. Dalio generated this performance ONLY with his own money, he'd be nowhere near as wealthy as the $22 billion he is worth today. Let me explain…

Let's imagine that Mr. Dalio somehow managed to scrounge together $1 million prior to starting his professional investing career. Without the assistance of Other People's Money, based on his historic track record, after 28 years Mr. Dalio would be worth… **$21 million.**

Yes, you read that correctly. Take away his clients' money, assume Mr. Dalio started off with $1 million and never added to that amount, and he'd be worth $21 million nearly 30 years later. True, $21 million is serious money. But it's nowhere near the $22 billion he's worth courtesy of using Other People's Money.

Obviously, no one would start with $1 million in investing and never add to their capital, especially if they discover they can beat the market consistently. So, let's now assume that Mr. Dalio added $5,000 per month or $60,000 per year to his initial $1 million throughout the course of his career. **<u>Under these circumstances, with the same extraordinary track record he'd be worth $32 million after 28 years.</u>**

Again, that is quite rich, but it's run-of-the-mill rich, not *"one of the wealthiest, most powerful people in the world"* rich.

Now let's get REALLY crazy with this example.

Let's say that Mr. Dalio was able to do MUCH better with his investing performance, averaging an incredible 30% a year for 28 years (something perhaps a handful of people have done), while adding $5,000 per month or $60,000 per year to his initial $1 million...

Using these numbers, Mr. Dalio would be worth ~$2 billion after 28 years.

Now we're talking about legitimate super wealth. But it's less than 10% of what Mr. Dalio has made using other people's money. And bear in mind, we're assuming he was THREE TIMES better at investing than he really is... and beating the market by SIX-FOLD for nearly three decades straight!

Of course, I'm being a bit unfair to Mr. Dalio here. The reality is that anyone who can outperform the stock market for decades, let alone double the stock market's performance, is going to attract a LOT of capital from outside investors.

However, the point remains, the reason he became a billionaire and one of the wealthiest, most powerful people in the world is because of Other People's Money.

Also, note again that we're talking about someone who got rich from the markets over the course of DECADES, not weeks or months. Which returns us to my original point... **there is no such thing as getting rick quickly from the markets**. Anyone who got rich *quickly* from the markets did so by:

1. Getting lucky.

2. Using other people's money.

3. Most likely a combination of #1 and #2.

Having said that, you *can* generate life-changing wealth from the markets... but it doesn't happen quickly.

It also requires two things.

1. Knowing who you are as an investor.

2. Never veering away from the strategies that work best for you; unless, of course, you decide that you want to become more serious about investing and are willing to devote the thousands of hours required to do so.

There is No Magic Formula or One-Size-Fits-All Strategy

Investing is a *very* specific enterprise. What works for one investor won't work for another.

If you spend even a few hours reading about the investing legends, you'll quickly discover that they all invest differently. Warren Buffett's investment style is nothing like that of Stanley Druckenmiller, whose investment style is nothing like that of Jim Rogers, whose investment style is nothing like that of Carl Icahn.

There is a reason for this. Investing is a very personal thing. The notion that there is some kind of formula for making money from the markets is completely misguided. In fact, there are as many ways of making money from the markets as there are people who invest.

Let me give you a brief example.

Below is a weekly chart for Apple's (AAPL) stock price over the last three years. Each one of those bars represents the price action of an entire week.

Chart 12: Apple, Inc. Share Price (2021-2024)

Note: Chart courtesy of StockCharts.com

There are literally dozens of different strategies investors might employ to profit from this stock.

Firstly, AAPL is one of the largest companies in the market. It's also one of the most-owned stocks in the world. In this context, a totally passive investor (someone who owns a stock-based retirement fund and never even bothers to see what's in it) would likely have some exposure to AAPL simply by virtue of having exposure to the stock market. That person profited from AAPL's rise in share price without even knowing he or she owned it!

By way of contrast, an active value investor (someone who actively manages his or her brokerage or retirement account) might have noted that AAPL was "cheap" based on any number of valuation metrics (Price to Earnings, Price to Cash Flow, etc.) during the pandemic and loaded up on shares. This person also profited from AAPL's rise, though his or her investment was based on specific criteria: AAPL was cheap relative to its historical valuation.

Still another method of profiting from AAPL's stock during the period illustrated in the above chart would consist of actively trading AAPL shares based on momentum, or the relative strength of AAPL's stock compared to the rest of the stock market. Unlike the passive investor or value investor we've already described, the momentum-based trader would have moved in and out of AAPL over relatively short periods of time (days or weeks) rather than simply buying shares and then holding on to them for a prolonged period.

Still yet another method of profiting from AAPL's rise in share price in the above chart consists of trading historical or seasonal patterns. An active trader might note that AAPL shares tend to rise into its earnings announcements, whenever the company unveils a new product, or during the last three months of the year (October to December). Our seasonal-centric active trader, like the momentum trader already described, would move in and out of AAPL shares over short periods of time based on these historic or seasonal patterns rather than simply "buying and holding" the stock.

I'm going to stop here, but there are literally dozens of other strategies an investor or trader could employ to profit from AAPL's stock. And bear in mind, the above examples concern only one single investment: Apple. There are thousands of companies, a dozen different asset classes and countless types of derivatives you can trade in any number of combinations!

Again, investing is a **very personal thing**. For this reason, the #1 issue for any investor is to figure out what kind of investor he or she is. Bear in mind there are NO WRONG ANSWERS to that inquiry. You simply need to take an honest assessment of you who are.

How to Assess Who You Are As An Investor

Investing is a complicated thing that involves a myriad of factors. To assess who you are as an investor you need to assess...

1. Who you are physically/logistically:
    a. Your age
    b. Your relative health
    c. The time you have available to analyze and monitor potential investments

2. Who you are psychologically:
    a. Your mental health
    b. Your ability to handle stress
    c. Are you stubborn and determined or are you passive and patient when it comes to getting what you want?
    d. Are you naturally an optimist or a pessimist?

3. Your relationship with money:
    a. Do you feel as if you have enough, or do you need more?
    b. Does handling money stress you out?

    c.   Are you comfortable taking risks with money or are you risk averse?

4. Your sophistication as an investor:
    a.   Are you a total novice when it comes to the markets?
    b.   Have you been investing for a little while (months)?
    c.   Have you been investing for a long time (years)?

5. Your interest level in investing:
    a.   Are you extremely interested in learning more about investing/trading?
    b.   How important is it to you for you to be successful at investing/trading?
    c.   How much time and effort are you willing to commit to your investing/trading goals?

… as well as a myriad of other items.

Again, there are no wrong answers to these questions. All you're doing is developing your profile as an investor. And while there are literally hundreds, if not thousands of investment styles and strategies, most individual investors (non-professionals) fall into two main categories.

They are:

1. Passive

    Or,

2. Active

Passive investors are "buy and hold" investors in that their exposure to the markets is usually measured in terms of months if not years or even decades.

These folks are usually involved in the markets via stock-based retirement accounts (401(k)s or IRAs) as opposed to self-directed brokerage accounts. Put another way, they don't open individual brokerage accounts to try to time the markets on a regular basis; rather they have their money in an investment fund or funds that are managed by others.

Passive investors rarely, if ever, open or close positions. The stocks they own are usually owned through a fund, meaning they didn't pick the investments themselves. And they typically don't monitor the markets unless something dramatic happens and the stock market grabs headlines.

There is nothing wrong with being a passive investor. Indeed, there is ample evidence that passive investing outperforms active investing most of the time. The reason for this is that historically, stocks tend to go up over time. Yes, there are bear markets or periods in which stocks as a whole go down, sometimes for several years. But overall, particularly over long periods of time (decades), stocks usually go up.

Passive investing profits from this.

Active investors are just that: active. They attempt to "time the markets" to produce significant gains. This can mean anything from making several trades a year to even several trades per day. Their understanding of the markets is usually more sophisticated than that of passive investors. And their retirement or brokerage accounts are usually self-directed meaning they are the person choosing to buy or sell a given investment.

Active investing is hard. But, if done correctly, an active investor can potentially make a LOT of money over the long-term. We'll delve into how to do this later, but the simplest way of thinking about active investing is that it involves taking on more risk as well as the potential for a LOT more reward.

Determining whether you are a passive or active investor ultimately boils down to how much time you can reasonably commit to the markets.

1. If you rarely check the markets, rarely buy or sell a stock (think less than five transactions per year) and typically spend less than a few hours a week on market analysis, you are most likely a passive investor.

2. If you frequently check the markets, frequently buy and sell stocks (you make 10 or more transactions a year) and often spend hours a week thinking about or analyzing the markets, you are most likely an active investor.

Again, there are NO wrong answers here. There are plenty of passive investors who perform better than active investors just as there are plenty of active investors who perform better than passive investors. All that matters is knowing what type of investor you are. After that, the most important thing is to **NEVER veer away from an investment/ trading strategy that plays to your strengths and minimizes your weaknesses.**

Why?

Having spent my entire adult life working in the investment field, I can say that the #1 thing that differentiates successful investors from those who lose money is **discipline.**

The fact is that the stock market is extremely volatile. It is not unusual for a stock to rise or fall 20% or more in a week. It is this volatility that opens the door to extraordinary profits.

However, volatility is *extremely* difficult to handle, especially if it means making or losing money, sometimes quite rapidly. Risking money makes people emotional. And being emotional, particularly in a volatile situation, is a recipe for losses. Indeed, in its simplest rendering, the problem with how most people invest can be illustrated in the following equation:

Volatility + Emotions + Money = Poor Decision Making.

Investing discipline concerns how you deal with volatility and emotionality. It, combined with your knowledge of who you are as an investor, is what will guide you through the markets successfully.

With that in mind, the remainder of this book will be devoted to outlining some real-world tools you can use to navigate the stock market, whether you are a passive or active investor.

I am focusing exclusively on stocks because:

1. They are the most-owned asset class (outside of real estate) with some 56% of American households having exposure to the stock market in one form or another.

2. Investing in commodities, bonds, and other asset classes requires highly specialized knowledge that is outside the scope of this book.

Let's dig in!

CHAPTER 5

Introduction to Stocks

No OTHER ASSET class garners as much attention, or as much excitement (except for crypto currencies) as stocks. However, in the grand scheme of things, the stock market is a relatively small market.

Depending on stock price levels, the total value of the U.S. stock market (the largest in the world) is about $20-$50 trillion in size. At the time of this writing, U.S. stocks are worth about $50 trillion. By way of contrast, the U.S. debt or credit markets are nearly double this at $98 trillion. And the currency markets dwarf even the debt markets.

It's impossible to know the precise size of the currency markets because currencies trade in pairs (meaning you are always selling one currency to buy another). But the daily market volume for the currency markets is over $6 trillion per day. To put that number into context, stocks trade about $232 billion per day. So, the currency markets, by volume, **are roughly 25 times larger than the stock market.**

Despite their small size, stocks get almost all the attention from the media and public. One reason for this is because most Americans' retirements are closely aligned with stock levels: some 56% of Americans own stocks, mostly via 401(k)s and other retirement accounts. And outside of their homes, the vast majority of American household's net worth is stored in stocks.

The other reason stocks get so much attention is because they have much higher volatility than bonds or currencies. It is unusual for a currency, particularly a developed nation's currency, to move more than 2% in a single day, whereas it is not unusual for an individual stock to move 10%, 50% or even 100% in a single day.

Also, stocks generally offer the best opportunity for creating generational wealth for most people (outside of real estate). By buying the best companies and holding for decades, an investor can see a return on capital of 10,000% or even 100,000%.

Again, those returns come from buying *the best companies*. But even if an investor were to buy a stock market index and hold for the course or his or her lifetime, he or she could potentially see much greater returns than if he or she were to put his or her money into bonds, real estate, or a Certificate of Deposit (CD).

However, despite their popularity, stocks are not well understood by most people outside the financial industry. Sure, most people can name a few stocks like Apple or Tesla… but do they really know what they are talking about?

So, let's start with the very basics.

What Is a Stock?

When people talk about a stock, they are referring to "equity in a publicly traded company."

What is equity?

Equity is a class of ownership. When you "buy a stock" you are buying an **ownership stake** in the company's business. This is why Warren Buffett is described as "owning" Coca-Cola, because he owns 10% of its equity shares.

Most of the time, when someone talks about stocks or equities, they are referring to "publicly traded equities," or companies that are publicly traded via a stock exchange such as the NASDAQ or the New York Stock Exchange. Publicly traded companies typically start out as privately held businesses (more on this later) that decide to "go public" meaning they will make shares in the business available to the general public.

To do this, the company would hire a Wall Street firm to stage an Initial Public Offering (IPO) through which shares in the company would begin to trade on one of the public stock exchanges: the NASDAQ, the S&P 500, the New York Stock Exchange, etc. During this process, the company would pick a one- to four-letter stock symbol that would be used to track its performance, e.g., Apple is AAPL, Tesla is TSLA, Visa is V, etc. Once the company goes public (unless the company is taken private again or goes bankrupt) the company's shares are available to buy or sell every Monday through Friday from 9:30 AM to 4 PM Eastern Standard Time in the U.S. (unless there's a federal holiday).

Why go public?

First and foremost, publicly traded companies usually trade at a higher valuation than privately held business. Private businesses usually are priced at anywhere from two to three, or maybe six times their annual profits. So, if ABC company produces $5 million in profits per year, the most you'd expect a private buyer to be willing to pay for the firm would be $30 million (and frankly that's a very rich valuation).

By way of comparison, publicly traded companies, because it's easy to buy and sell their shares, are priced at much higher price multiples. It is not uncommon for a publicly traded company to trade at 20, 30 or even 50 times their profits. In fact, quite a few publicly traded companies are

Graham Summers, MBA

valued at hundreds of millions of dollars, and they've never produced a cent in profits!

Obviously, if you're a private owner of a business, taking it public offers you the opportunity to have your ownership stake valued at a MUCH higher amount.

Another reason to take a company public is because it provides much greater liquidity. Shares in privately held businesses rarely if ever change hands. By way of comparison, shares of publicly traded companies trade every second of every weekday between 9:30AM and 4PM EST. So, if you are the private owner of a business, taking it public offers you the ability to sell your shares much more easily: all you have to do is open your brokerage account and hit "sell." By way of contrast, to sell shares in a privately held business you'd have to line up an actual buyer and have a lawyer write up a contract for the sale: a process that can be both quite slow and expensive. Put simply, publicly traded companies are much more liquid and typically trade at higher valuations.

I mentioned before that an equity is an ownership class. It is in fact the most junior ownership class for a company, behind creditors. So, if a company that you own goes bankrupt, it will first pay off the people and institutions to which it owes money before you get a portion of anything that is left over. The process is obviously much more complicated than this, but it's worth mentioning that stockholders are the lowest on the totem pole in terms of ownership of a company's assets and underlying business.

Why Own a Stock?

There are two reasons to own a stock:

1. You hope to sell your shares to someone else at a higher price (capital gains).

2. You hope to receive a portion of the business' cash flows (dividends).

The first option is essentially speculation: you are buying shares in the company not for any intrinsic value, nor because you want to own a part of its business, but simply because you believe its price will rise and you will be able to sell your shares to someone else at a higher price.

There are plenty of fundamental and technical reasons to do this. Perhaps you believe the company is going to announce a new product that will excite investors. Or perhaps the company's shares have strong upwards momentum meaning that buying demand is outpacing selling supply and shares are moving up in price. Whatever the reason, you are not buying and holding your position in the stock for the long-term, you are simply speculating that its price will rise in the short-term at which point you plan to sell your shares at a profit.

Regarding #2, this is akin to the "Warren Buffett style" of investing: you are buying a share in the company because you believe in its underlying business. You believe that over time the company will grow significantly, resulting in larger profits that the company will hopefully pay out to you in the form of dividends.

In this scenario, you are not looking to sell your shares soon, if ever. You are not interested in producing a quick profit, nor do you care if shares lose value in the near-term. You are a business *owner*, not a speculator. For most investors, this is how true generational wealth can be created.

Let's use a real-world example here.

One of Warren Buffett's largest positions is Coca-Cola (NYSE: KO). He first bought shares of the company in 1988 and 1989 when they were trading round $43.81 per share (they've since undergone numerous stock splits, so the adjusted share price is now $2.73).

In Coca-Cola, Buffett saw an incredible business that he believed would grow dramatically in the future. Some items he noted:

1. Coke hadn't changed the formula to its famous drink much since it was invented in 1886. This was a product that had already lasted 100 years.

2. You can drink six cokes a day and not get sick of the taste. Practically no other beverage or food item shares this quality (imagine eating six chocolate bars every day).

3. Coke is an inflation-proof business: the company can raise the price of a can of soda time and again without hurting demand.

Buffett was correct on all counts, particularly Coke's growth prospects. In 1988, when Buffett first began buying Coca-Cola's stock, the company produced $8 billion in annual revenue. In 2023, the company produced ~$45 billion in annual revenue.

Moreover, historically Coca-Cola's management has focused on increasing returns to shareholders (people who own its stock) in the form of its dividends. Coke has increased its dividend every year for 60 years. Based on Buffett's original buy price ($2.73), and the company's 2022 dividend ($1.76), he is locking in a ~64% return on his original purchase on an **annual basis** via dividends alone!

Buffett has also seen the value of his shares rise over 4,500%. Had you followed Warren Buffett into this investment and bought 100 shares of Coca-Cola in 1988, the initial cost would have been $2,450. Today, that same stake would be worth $40,000. And if you had chosen to *reinvest* your dividends, meaning you used them to buy more shares of Coke's stock, your 100 shares would be worth **$80,426.**

This returns us to my primary point concerning investing… you *can* get FILTHY rich from stocks, but the process takes *years,* if not decades to occur. The key is to know who you are as an investor, NEVER veer away from the strategy that plays to your strengths, and for 99% of investors, invest for the long-term.

Why for the long-term?

Because unless you are willing to spend thousands of hours learning about the markets all while losing thousands of dollars as part of your "education," your best bet in terms of seeing extraordinary returns is to buy and hold for years.

Welcome to the world of passive investing!

CHAPTER 6

Strategies for Passive Investors

As I MENTIONED in the introduction to this portion of the book, passive investing involves buying and holding stocks for a prolonged period: usually years, if not decades.

Your typical passive investor is someone who has stock market exposure via a stock-based retirement account (a 401(k) or IRA). He or she often doesn't know what specific stocks or bonds are in the account. And aside from the occasional review of the account at quarter or year-end, a passive investor usually doesn't give it much thought (unless something dramatic happens that makes the stock market front page news).

On the surface, passive investing sounds weak or feeble. Even the word "passive" sounds as if the person involved is incapable of making a decision. Do not let this fool you. There is ample evidence that passive investors frequently outperform active investors by a **wide margin.** To understand why this is, let's first consider some facts about the markets and how investors tend to get in their own way when it comes to making money.

Fact #1: Over the Long Term, Stocks Go Up Most of the Time

In some ways, the stock market is the closest thing we have to a discounting mechanism for human innovation. Every company on the stock market was founded by someone who invented something: a new good or service, a new means of delivering a good or service, or some improved version of a prior technology.

In short, most stocks represent some version of human creation or innovation. Obviously, there are exceptions to this, but the stock market, taken as a whole, is the closest thing you have to "betting" on human ingenuity.

This is particularly true when you consider that typically inferior companies with inferior products and services end up failing. Those companies are eventually removed from the stock market indices. So, when you buy the stock market, you are effectively buying the "winners" in the economy.

Now, humans get a lot of things wrong. But when it comes to innovation and economic development, it's generally not a good idea to bet against us. And for this reason, the stock market *generally* tends to go up.

Some data points to consider... Over the last 100 years, the stock market has risen more than two out of every three years (68% of the time to be precise). And since 1928, the stock market has gone up an average of 9% per year (this includes losing years).

In this context, putting your money into the stock market tends to be a winning proposition for passive investors. Firstly, there is a 68% chance that the stock market is going to finish the year with a gain. And secondly, provided you hold for the long term, the odds greatly favor you making money as opposed to losing it. For this reason alone, a passive investor who puts his or her money into the stock market via a retirement account and waits is more likely to do better than someone who attempts to actively time the market.

Why is this?

Because few if any investors actually beat the market in the long term. Yes, there are investors who can beat the market for years on end, but they are the exception, NOT the rule. According to *Bloomberg*[2] there are roughly 2,850 actively managed U.S. stock mutual funds. In any given year, only a little over a third of them will beat the market. Of those funds, only 17% will beat the market for 10 years, and only 6% will beat the market over 20 years.

Put another way, even professional investors, who spend most of their waking hours focused on the markets and who have entire research teams assisting them, rarely beat the market for long: again, at best a little over one in three of them will do so on any given year, and less than one in five will do so over a decade.

Already you can see how being a passive investor gives you a distinct advantage: you barely have to do any work and you will typically outperform four out of five professionals in the long-term.

Why is this?

Fact #2: The More Frequently You Check Your Portfolio, the Worse Your Performance Will Be

Handling money is an emotional thing. And the volatility of the stock market amplifies this dramatically.

The average daily stock market move is ~1%. That doesn't sound like much… but for a portfolio of $1,000,000, a 1% move means making or losing $10,000. And bear in mind, that's just the *average* daily move. It is not uncommon to see multiple daily moves of 2%, 3%, or even 5% in any

---

2   https://www.bloomberg.com/opinion/articles/2022-05-31/active-managers-are-having-a-moment-that-won-t-last

given year. And during extreme situations, the stock market can move as much as 10% or even 15% during a single day.

Now, we're talking about a significant amount of capital disappearing in just 24 hours. Imagine the investor who put most of his or her retirement account into a stock index over the course of his or her career waking up on October 20th, 1987, to discover that he or she had lost 22% of their retirement in the Black Monday Crash the day before.

And bear in mind, we are talking about the stock market as a whole here. Individual stocks are much more volatile, with daily price moves of 5% or more being quite common. And if you mess around with microcap ("penny" stocks), it's quite normal to see a company move double and even triple digits in a week!

Put simply: stocks are an *extremely* volatile asset class. And this volatility means potentially making or losing a LOT of money in a short period of time. This is especially true if you are not careful with your position sizing (we will address this topic in greater detail in the next chapter).

Let me give you an example.

Let's say you are a novice investor who has saved up $25,000 to invest. Given that you are a novice, you will likely put *way* too much of your money into a single stock (20% or $5,000) hoping for some nice returns.

However, unfortunately for you the company you bought reports disappointing earnings a week later, and **its stock plunges 20% in a single day.** You just lost $1,000, or 4% of your entire portfolio. In a single day.

"Sure thing, Graham," you might be thinking, *"but only small, risky companies drop 20% in a single day. So, this example is really not a good one."*

In 2022, Amazon, Meta (formerly Facebook), Target, and Netflix all experienced single day drops that were 20% or larger. All of them were valued at over $100 BILLION at the time they did this.

Again, stocks are a volatile asset class. This volatility means your portfolio can either make or lose a LOT of money in a short period of time. That means a LOT of stress and emotions for the investor trying to navigate the markets. High amounts of stress and emotions are NOT conducive to good decision-making. And in investing, **bad decision-making = losing money.**

This is one of several reasons why numerous studies have illustrated that the more frequently an investor checks his or her portfolio, the worse he or she will fare as an investor. This makes sense particularly in the context of the first fact we laid out in this chapter: stocks tend to go up over time.

If stocks tend to go up, but are very volatile, then someone who frequently checks on the market is far more likely to get overly emotional and sell or buy at the wrong time, thereby costing him- or herself substantial gains as stocks eventually work higher over time. In this sense, passive investors have a distinct advantage over their active counterparts due to the fact that passive investors typically don't look at the market often.

So why isn't everyone a passive investor? After all, it sounds like the ideal approach with less stress and better portfolio performance!

Two reasons:

1. There are prolonged periods in which the market doesn't go **anywhere**.

2. When the market collapses, it tends to erase several years' worth of gains quite quickly.

Regarding #1, the below chart shows the 100-year performance of the Dow Jones Industrial Average. This is a log chart to make up for the fact that the Dow has moved so much higher over the last century.

Chart 13: Dow Jones Industrial Average (1920-2024)

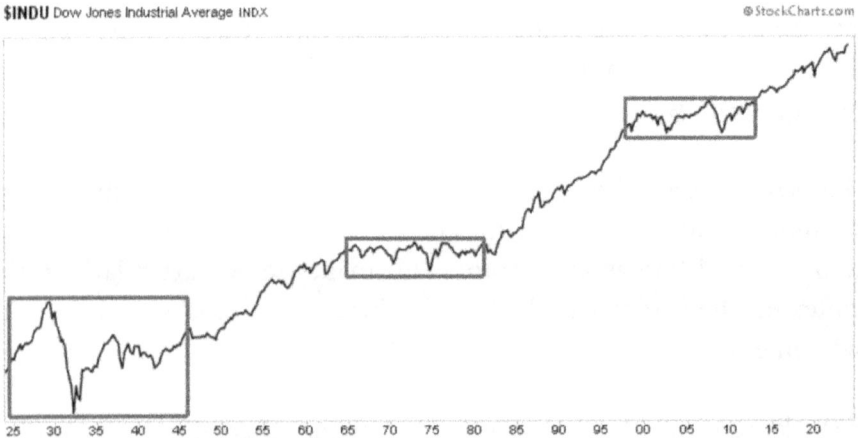

Note: Chart courtesy of StockCharts.com

As you can see, there have been multiple periods during which stocks spent a decade or more moving sideways. I've highlighted those periods with rectangles. They were:

- 1925-1945 (20 years)
- 1965-1982 (17 years)
- 1997-2013 (16 years)

Now, it's tempting to look at this chart and say, *"sure, there are times when stocks go nowhere, but once those periods end, the market rips higher and doesn't look back. So, all you need to do is wait it out."*

Technically, this is correct. However, the odds of someone willingly sitting on portfolio losses (some of which are massive) for **20 years** is next to zero. A real human being with real money in the markets would despair in these situations. Remember, we're talking about periods of 20 YEARS in which stocks go nowhere.

This isn't ancient history, either. The passive investor who started a 401(k) at age 23 in 1997 didn't see a CENT in profits from the markets until he or she was almost 40 in 2013. Put another way, the only increase he or she saw in his or her 401(k) during this period was from the payroll deposits, NOT the markets!

Of course, the reality is that our passive investor likely wouldn't have remained passive for too long in this environment. As I've emphasized repeatedly in this chapter, the volatility of the stock market makes investors emotional. And the reality is that few if any investors could have stomached the Tech Crash from 2000-2003, nor the Great Financial Crisis of 2007-2009 without selling everything.

Which brings me to the second reason why passive investing doesn't always work: when the market *does* collapse, it tends to erase several years' worth of gains quite quickly.

Consider the Great Financial Crisis of 2008... During the preceding bull market, stocks as measured by the S&P 500 roughly doubled in value from April 2003 until their peak in November 2007. This was a period of EXTRAORDINARY gains in which stocks rose nearly 25% per year on average.

During the Great Financial Crisis, the markets erased ALL of these gains and then some in the span of just 14 months. That's more than FOUR YEARS' worth of gains erased in less than a year and a half. And the markets wouldn't reach new highs following the crisis until **2013.**

So again, the biggest drawbacks to passive investing are that:

1. There are prolonged periods in which the stock market doesn't go anywhere.

2. When the stock market collapses, it tends to erase several years' worth of gains quite quickly.

With the above items in mind, the key for any passive investor is to ride a bull market for as long as possible, and then sell to avoid the drawdowns of bear markets. Put another way, a passive investor needs to focus on just one thing:

Avoiding the busts.

If a buy-and-hold investor bought the S&P 500 and rode the booms of 1991-2000, 2003-2007, and 2009 until today, while AVOIDING the busts of 2000-2003 and 2007-2009, he or she would have made a fortune.

Using the S&P 500 as a proxy for the stock market, our buy-and-hold investor would have made 450% during the boom of the 1990s, another 100%+ during the boom of 2003-2007, and another 500+% during the boom from 2009 until early-2024 (the time of this writing). And thanks to the miracle of compounding, every $1,000 invested in 1991 would be worth over $40,000 today.

And if our buy-and-hold investor continued adding to his or her nest egg throughout this time period... perhaps to the tune of $1,000 every month, he or she would be a MULTI-MILLIONAIRE.

Best of all, a buy-and-hold investor wouldn't need to predict anything to do this. He or she wouldn't need to follow what the Fed was doing, read financial statements, watch CNBC or anything else. ALL he or she would need to do is AVOID the BUSTS.

So how do you do this?

One metric that works well is to use the 48-Month Moving Average (MMA) as a guide for when to get in or out of stocks. If you're unfamiliar with a moving average, all it does is illustrate the market's average price over a particular period (in this case, 48 months, or four years) as a line.

Below is a chart of the S&P 500 with this line running back the late 1980s. As you can see, stocks tend to "respect" this line to a great degree, "bouncing" off this level during bull markets and only breaking below it during bear markets (remember, the line is not an actual physical barrier, it's simply a visual representation of the average price of the market's levels during the prior 48 months).

Chart 14: Standard & Poor's 500 (1982-2024)

$SPX S&P 500 Large Cap Index INDX   © StockCharts.com

Note: Chart courtesy of StockCharts.com

Using this metric as a means of risk management would mean selling stocks anytime the market falls below the 48-MMA on a monthly basis (meaning you waited until the end of a calendar month for confirmation of a break) and buying them anytime they move above this line on a monthly basis (ditto).

If you did this over the last 30 years, you would have caught the bulk of most bull markets while missing the bulk of most bear markets as the below chart illustrates.

Chart 15: Standard & Poor's 500 (1982-2024)

Note: Chart courtesy of StockCharts.com

The reason I like this tool is because it's a long-term metric, meaning the market has to make a MAJOR change in trend for a buy or sell signal to be triggered. This allows a buy-and-hold investor who simply wants to profit from stocks without spending a ton of time watching the markets to catch the bulk of most major trends.

Bear in mind, this tool is not perfect (nothing in investing is perfect). And there are some environments in which an investor would be relatively busy due to selling his or her stocks only to then buy back again a few months later. One such period occurred from 1950-1970. However, even then this strategy would help you avoid big losses... and you'd still eke out some decent gains at the same time.

However, for the most part, the 48-MMA is an excellent risk management tool for the long-term passive investor. It's simple, requires next to no work, and is highly effective. Best of all, you can use any basic charting service to do it.

This concludes our chapter on passive investing strategies. For those who are interested in beating the market, potentially by quite a lot, we will need to introduce other strategies as well as a more robust investing framework.

Welcome to the world of active investing!

CHAPTER 7

On Active Stock Market Investing

As I MENTIONED earlier in this book, active investors attempt to outperform the market via investing strategies that require moving in and out of stocks more frequently than passive stock investors. Active stock investing is actually one of the most diverse fields of investing. Just off the top of my head there are:

1. Value investors: investors who try to buy a company when it is trading at a share price that is below the intrinsic value of its underlying businesses.

2. Momentum investors: investors who use various metrics to identify stocks that are about to become more popular with other investors and therefore rally.

3. Macro investors: investors who use macroeconomic data and price action in other asset classes to determine whether stocks should rally or fall.

4. Technical analysis investors: investors who use chart patterns and other metrics to identify stocks that are about to move sharply higher or sharply lower in the short-term.

5. Stock option investors: investors who trade derivatives that offer them the right to buy or sell stocks at specific prices at some point in the future.

You get the idea.

And bear in mind, each of the categories I've outlined above have numerous sub-segments of investors who approach these methods of investing from different perspectives or frameworks. Indeed, you could safely argue that *every* active investor has his or her own specific method for investing in stocks. And any given investor might employ different strategies during the course of his or her career.

My point is that the subject of active stock investing could easily comprise a multi-volume set of books. And since there are already many great books on each of the above strategies, I'll be devoting most of this chapter to addressing some of the greatest challenges individual investors face when they embark on their active stock-investing journeys.

Put simply, the goal for this chapter is to help you learn to think about active stock investing differently so that you avoid making the major mistakes that individual investors typically make. Provided you do this, over time you should begin to make money and potentially a LOT of money from your stock investments.

Let's get started.

Stocks Are a *Risk* Asset

At their core, stocks are a **risk asset**. They are volatile, oftentimes irrational, and ever changing in their focus.

Think of it this way: at any given time, the market's action is determined by the decisions of millions of individuals, all of whom have "skin in the game" in the form of money. So, the market is processing literally billions, if not trillions, of pieces of information every day.

However, out of all these pieces of information, stocks usually only "care about" or focus on two or three items at any particular time. Sometimes it might be the economy. Other times it might be the Fed. Other times it might be a war, or a President's actions (or tweets), or a hedge fund blowing up, or inflation, etc.

For active stock investors who are looking to time or outperform the market, risk is everywhere. Every time you open your brokerage account to buy something there are numerous risks involved. Just off the top of my head there are:

1. The risk that you are buying at the wrong time, whether it be from a macro/ business cycle perspective or from the perspective of the company's business, e.g., its next product will be a dud, its business is starting to decline, etc.

2. The risk that you are buying at the wrong price, e.g., the company is too richly valued, an accounting scandal is about to hit the wires, the company is about to announce bad quarterly results, etc.

3. The risk that you are buying the wrong investment, of which there are two sub-risks:
   a. The risk that the investment is fundamentally a bad one (the company is a fraud, or a dinosaur, etc.) that will lose money for a prolonged period, possibly going to zero.
   b. The risk that there is another investment that will perform even better.

You get my point.

Given that investing in stocks involves taking on *considerable* risk, an active stock investor MUST always maintain some degree of **risk management** in order to succeed. The reason for this is that there is no such thing as a "risk free" stock. And while there are literally dozens of different risks an investor must deal with when he or she buys a stock, all of them ultimately fall into one or two categories:

1. The risk of missing out on gains.

   Or,

2. The risk of losing money.

Having been in the investing industry for 20 years, I believe the biggest mistake that most stock investors make is to focus too much on #1, instead of #2.

Put simply, almost everyone who gets involved in active stock investing does so hoping to get rich. Almost no one approaches a given stock from the perspective of *"how much money could I lose?"* And ironically, most individual investors usually end up doing just that: losing money or underperforming the market.

This lack of risk management is not entirely their fault.

The financial industry, to some degree, is designed to dangle some "hot stock tip" or "get rich quick" scheme in front of potential clients. After all, how many fund managers would successfully raise capital by saying, *"our goal is to NOT lose money"*? Moreover, the entire financial media complex (*CNBC, Bloomberg*, etc.), as well as the investing-focused areas of social media, focus on *potential profits and gains* rather than the risk of losing money.

Think about it. When was the last time someone on TV, or X (formerly

Twitter), or Facebook, or TikTok, talked about how much money you could *lose* on an investment instead of how much money you could make? I'd wager the answer is "**never**."

Why is this?

Because humans are greatly affected by their emotions. Thinking about losing money makes people afraid. And this makes them less likely to buy something. In contrast, thinking about *making money* gets people excited. And when people are excited, they are more likely to buy something. And the investing industry as a whole does better **when people want to buy something.**

The great irony here is that the investors who end up actually *making money* (and potentially a lot of it) from their stock investments, are almost always those who focus a great deal on the risk of losing money.

Why?

Because, as I outlined earlier in this chapter, investing in stocks is *__inherently risky__*. There is no such thing as a "risk free" stock investment. So, if your focus is on *how much money you could lose*, you are more focused on the reality of stock investing than the fantasy of future riches. As such, you will do a better job of avoiding catastrophic losses from your investments (more on this shortly).

Remember from the last chapter (*Strategies For Passive Investors*), over the long term stocks tend to go up. So, provided you avoid losing a LOT of money, the odds are in your favor that over time your portfolio will grow. And if you continue growing your portfolio without ever suffering a *catastrophic loss*, eventually your brokerage account will get to the size that even a small gain (say 5%) will mean making thousands, if not tens of thousands of dollars. And that is how you get rich from the stock market: over time and gradually.

This returns us to our first "Dirty Little Secret of Investing" from earlier in this book: **it is IMPOSSIBLE to get rich *quick* in investing.** Yes, there are people who might briefly accumulate wealth from their stock investments in a rapid fashion. But all of them end up losing their wealth just as rapidly. Indeed, the only person who can *successfully* get rich rapidly from investing is someone who "gets lucky" using a high-risk strategy and then immediately walks away from the markets, thereby ensuring they keep their gains. In 20 years, I've yet to meet anyone who has done this.

I realize this is likely quite disappointing. But it's the truth. If you want to get rich in active stock market investing, it's going to take a LOT of time and a lot of effort. Let's provide a little context here...

Trading the Stock Market is a Skilled Trade, Like Dentistry, Plumbing or Practicing Law

Any profession in which you can generate significant income takes *years* for you to get to the level at which it is possible to do so. Becoming a lawyer takes four years. Becoming a dentist takes six to eight years. Becoming a doctor can take 10 to 15 years depending on the specialty.

It's no different in the trade world either. Becoming a licensed tradesperson (HVAC, plumbing, etc.) takes five years. And if you want to make *real* money in the trades, you need to start your own business, which is a whole other type of "education."

So, if it takes hundreds of hours of training to make money practicing the law, dentistry, or plumbing, why would it take only a few hours or months to do so in the stock market... an environment in which literally everyone is competing with everyone else to make money?

My advice to anyone who wants to start actively investing in stocks is to think of it as a skilled trade like medicine or law. The big difference between stock market investing and any of the other trades I mentioned above is that there is practically no barrier to entry to becoming a stock investor. You don't need to obtain a specific degree, nor do you need to apprentice under someone more accomplished. All you need is the money required to open a brokerage account.

Moreover, unlike fixing toilets or treating patients, stock market investing is a relatively effortless task: the only real activity (aside from doing research or watching the markets) is when you hit "buy" or "sell" in your brokerage account. The rest of the time is spent reading, watching, learning or simply waiting.

I suspect it is the ease with which one can get into stock market investing, along with the financial media's focus on greed-triggering marketing campaigns, that makes so many people think they can "get rich quick" from the markets. But as I keep stating, you cannot. If you want to get rich from the markets, it will take considerable time, energy, and money. I mention money because, as I wrote earlier in this chapter, you *will* suffer losses in your journey to stock market success.

Moreover, losing money is something you will do for the entirety of your investing career. Yes, you will get better at investing over time. But you will never get to the point that you don't lose money anymore. The investing legends *still* make mistakes and lose money decades into their careers. So will you.

With all of the above items in mind, the single most important skill you need to develop (particularly if you're just starting out as an active investor) is to avoid suffering a catastrophic loss of capital.

Why? Because in investing, catastrophic losses are almost impossible to overcome.

First and foremost, few things are as depressing or upsetting as losing a lot of money. Losing a lot of money means feeling "worth less" emotionally as well as financially. And in investing, becoming emotional increases the odds of making mistakes and losing even more money.

Secondly, once you've suffered a big loss, your future investments will need to be even more profitable just for you to break even. For example, an investor who loses 25% of his or her portfolio needs to make 33% just to get back to where he or she was prior to the loss. This predicament only worsens as the size of the loss increases. A 50% loss on your portfolio means you need to DOUBLE your money to break even. A 75% loss on your portfolio means you need to TRIPLE your money to break even. And so on.

This is why Warren Buffett once famously said:

> *"The first rule of an investment is don't lose [money]. And the second rule of an investment is don't forget the first rule. And that's all the rules there are."*

Notice that Buffett didn't say, *"don't fight the Fed"* or *"buy great businesses"* or even *"buy at the bottom."* Instead, he said ***"don't lose money."***

Now, as I've repeated throughout this chapter, investing without losses is impossible. Every single investor in the world experiences losses. Indeed, Buffett himself has made multiple investments that lost him *billions* of dollars.

How do we resolve this contradiction?

What Warren Buffett is really saying in the above quote is that an investor's focus should be on "risk management," or the potential for losses, as opposed to the potential for gains. If you always account for potential losses, you approach an investment from a more rational, clear-thinking perspective.

How does one do this?

You can devote the next five or six years to following the markets closely until you are familiar enough with the ebb and flow of things that you develop your own risk management protocols. Or you could you use the ones I've developed during my 20-year career. They are:

1. Focus on high probability/low risk investments.

2. Carefully size your position.

3. Have an exit strategy or plan for when things work out, or don't.

Let's dive in.

CHAPTER 8

Strategies For Active Investors

As I MENTIONED at the end of the previous chapter, my framework for active stock market investing consists of three rules:

1. Focus on high probability/low risk investments.

2. Carefully size your position.

3. Have an exit strategy or plan for when things work out, or don't.

We'll work our way through all three of these in detail. If you can adopt these rules into your own investing, you'll avoid many of the mistakes most traders make.

Why You Should Focus on High Probability/Low Risk Investments

First and foremost, if you want to be successful as an active stock market investor, you should focus almost exclusively on **high probability trades**, meaning ones that have a high probability of working out.

I realize this sounds like a "duh" kind of statement to make. But you'd be amazed at how many stock investors assume outcomes that have a very **low probability** of happening.

Here again, it's not entirely their fault. The financial media and Hollywood LOVE the idea of the investor taking a long shot; betting on a "black swan" or some highly unusual development that will make the investor a fortune if it works. However, in real life, **these kinds of situations almost NEVER work.** At best these kinds of trades work out 0.00001% of the time.

I know right now you're probably thinking, *"sure thing, Graham, but what about movies like The Big Short where investors get filthy rich using special trades during a crash?"* Let me bring you in on a dirty little secret… **almost NO ONE made money during the market crashing in 2008.**

In 2008, there were roughly 216 million American adults over the age of 18. Roughly 60% of them had exposure to the stock market via brokerage accounts or stock-based retirements accounts (401(k)s, IRAs, etc.) So, we're talking about roughly **130 MILLION people** who were involved in the stock market in one form or another.

The number of investors who got rich betting on a crash at that time is under 30. So, we're talking about, at most, 30 people out of 130 MILLION getting rich from the crash. That's **roughly 0.00002%.** To put that into perspective, you are much more likely to be struck by lightning than to make a fortune from a crisis.

Moreover, those few investors who got rich from the Great Financial Crisis were all in **highly unusual** circumstances, none of which applied to the typical individual investor.

John Paulson is a famous hedge fund manager who became a billionaire betting on the housing crash. What you might not know is that the only reason he succeeded was because he *personally* had Goldman Sachs build securities that were chock full of garbage mortgages, which Goldman Sachs then sold to other clients… **so Paulson could bet *against them.***

This was unethical and borderline illegal. And individual investors like you or I would NEVER have this opportunity (when was the last time Goldman Sachs created something for you to bet against?).

Michael Burry is another hedge fund manager who got rich from betting on the housing crash. He had to lose money for two years before his bets worked out. And once things went in his favor, the investment banks who sold him the securities that he used to bet against the housing market **refused to mark his trades as being profitable.**

To top it off, his investors tried to withdraw their funds. When Burry refused to give the money back, **they sued him**. What followed was several years of legal hell as well as an investigation by the FBI, (not into the banks that sold the toxic mortgage securities to investors, but into Burry himself). Go figure.

So, let us consider this…

1. The odds of making a fortune betting on a crisis or some other black swan are less than those of being struck by lightning.

2. The small handful of people who *DO* get rich from these situations do so either because they have A) an unethical set up like John Paulson or B) are willing to experience a nightmarish scenario for months, or even years like Michael Burry.

So how do you make money in the stock market? By focusing on high probability trades: ones that have a higher probability of working out.

What is a High Probability Trade?

What qualifies as a high probability trade will depend on your profile as an investor. A high probability setup for a deep-value long-term investor will be very different from a high probability setup for a short-term momentum trader.

If you are a deep-value investor or an investor who tries to buy companies that are undervalued and hold them for months if not years, a high probability investment will be one in which you:

1. Have an expert understanding of the business: its leadership, operations, products, etc.

2. Performed a thorough review of its financial situation and growth prospects.

3. Have a setup that suggests its shares are ready to move higher in price.

Doing this amount of due diligence will weed out most of the low probability/high risk situations in your investing universe. And while there's no guarantee that you won't be wrong on a specific investment, having performed this much work will greatly reduce the odds that you will be **catastrophically wrong**.

By way of contrast, if you are a short-term momentum trader, meaning your time horizon is measured in weeks, not months or years, then a high probability investment will be one in which you:

1. Have been studying the company's chart or price action for some time to the point of having a solid understanding of how it trades.

2. Have a number of technical metrics that are working in your

favor (you're not just buying the trade at an arbitrary time with an arbitrary setup).

3. Have reviewed the company's corporate calendar to ensure that there isn't some major event about to occur that could negate your analysis (quarterly results announcements, product announcements, and investor days are all times during which a company's share price can go bananas, negating even the most convincing trade setups).

While I cannot possibly outline all the "high probability" setups for every type of investor here, the primary point I'm making is that when it comes time to hit "buy" on an investment, **you need to have done your homework.** Put another way, you should NEVER randomly buy something without having done considerable research on the investment in question.

I can assure you that NONE of the investing legends buy ANYTHING based solely on a hunch or a gut feeling. **These people always know what they own or know why they are buying it.** Moreover, all of them have been active in the markets long enough that this kind of framework is automatically built into their investment process.

Mind you, the "know what you own" method is true even for systems-based traders/ investors who perform quantitative analysis, trend following, or some other automated method of investing. Sure, these types of investors might not know a lot about the businesses that their systems are buying, **but they know their trading systems inside and out**, including the reasons why their systems are flagging those stocks as potential "buys."

Ultimately, my point is this: there are no "lazy" or "easy methods" to becoming a successful investor. If you want to make serious money from the markets, you will need to put in serious work, just as a medical student or law student must hit the books to earn the degree that allows them to earn a significant income.

I realize the above analysis is pretty general in nature, so let me give you an example of how to turn what appears to be a random investment into one with setups of various probabilities. The following example would apply to someone who is performing short-term trading.

A Sample Reading of Price Action

Below is a weekly chart for Apple (AAPL) depicting the company's price action over a period of 18 months (late 2021 to early 2023). Each bar represents the price movement of a week. White bars represent "up" weeks while black bars represent "down" weeks.

Chart 16: Apple, Inc. Share Price (2021-2023)

Note: Chart courtesy of StockCharts.com

Just looking at this chart, there appears to be no real trend. AAPL shares traded in a range between approximately $130 per share to $180 per share. At best you can say that the trading action has been choppy with no real direction or perhaps a slight downward bias. Thus, a superficial view of this chart suggests no high probability setups.

Now let's look at this same chart with a more analytical eye for setups based on probability and prior price action.

First and foremost, AAPL's price movements have some pretty clear parameters: a small weekly move sees AAPL shares move about $5, while a larger weekly move sees AAPL shares move $10-$12. The largest weekly move I see in the period of 18 months occurred in late October 2022 when AAPL shares dropped $20 in a single week.

Using the above information as the foundation for a trading framework, it is clear that a price movement of $12 or more in a given week is **un-likely**. Put another way, trading with the expectation of a $30 price move occurring in a single week is a **high risk/low probability trade.**

Looking more at this chart, you might notice another significant item: the price action upwards for AAPL is very different from the price movement down. Upwards moves have no real consistency. They can be anywhere from two to eight weeks in duration and can include multiple up weeks back-to-back or a combination of up and down weeks that ultimately see AAPL shares finish $40 higher.

I've illustrated the up moves in grey rectangles in the chart below.

Chart 17: Apple, Inc. Share Price (2021-2023)

Note: Chart courtesy of StockCharts.com

By way of contrast, downward moves in AAPL stock are fairly consistent during this 18-month period: they usually last four or more weeks in length. And while there might be an up week or two in the mix, those up weeks are usually relatively weak i.e. AAPL's shares don't bounce much. Simply put, if AAPL shares have a significant down week e.g. a drop in share price of ~$10 or more, the odds are relatively high that the next week will see AAPL shares under additional pressure.

I've illustrated the down moves in grey rectangles in the chart below.

Chart 18: Apple, Inc. Share Price (2021-2023)

Note: Chart courtesy of StockCharts.com

Building this into our trading framework, we can say that:

1. A weekly price movement of $5-$10 is a high probability for AAPL's stock. A price movement greater than that is a low probability outcome.

2. Upward price moves in AAPL tend to be inconsistent in length and scope and therefore more difficult to trade. This makes them lower probability setups.

3. Downward price moves in AAPL tend to be more consistent in length and scope and therefore easier to trade. This makes them higher probability setups.

You get the general idea: we've taken a rangebound stock and done enough homework to start isolating which setups have a higher probability of panning out.

Of course, if I was actively trading AAPL's stock with real money, I'd perform more analysis of its price action, with several more metrics (Bollinger Bands, Moving Averages, Support/ Resistance, etc.). And I'd also make sure there was a degree of fundamental analysis/ macro data to support my trades. However, the above outline serves as a decent introduction on how to think about price action when you look at a stock chart.

We've covered a lot of material here already, so let's do a brief recap before we continue to the next part of my investment framework (position sizing).

1. Investing in stocks ALWAYS involves a significant level of risk.

2. Because this risk never goes away, no matter how skilled you become as an investor, the single most important skill for an investor to develop is the ability to avoid catastrophic losses.

3. One means of avoiding a catastrophic loss is to perform significant research before making your investment decision. While this doesn't mean you'll always be right, it does reduce the odds of you being completely wrong and suffering a catastrophic loss.

    Some examples of research that can move the odds in your favor when it comes to investing:

a. Detailed and extensive knowledge of a company's underlying business.

b. Detailed and extensive knowledge concerning a stock's trading activity.

c. Some kind of specialized knowledge concerning the company's products, IP, etc. We all are experts on something, chances are there are publicly traded companies whose businesses are in your area of expertise.

Ultimately, the bottom-line is that you should focus on high probability/low risk trades and investments. There will be times during your career as an active investor in which you will make low probability/high risk trades, but MOST (as in more than 99%) of your trades should be in situations that have a high probability of working out.

This brings us to Rule #2 in my framework: **You MUST carefully size your position.**

What is Position Sizing and Why Does It Matter?

Position sizing is the skill through which an investor determines how much capital to risk in a given trade.

On the face of it, position sizing breaks down to a simple rule: **don't risk too much money**. However, as simple and straightforward as it sounds, position sizing might be the most important (and overlooked) aspect of trading. Indeed, I would wager than 99% of people who blow up their brokerage accounts do so because they used the wrong position size for a trade. This includes the investing legends, by the way.

Remember, in investing you are *guaranteed* to lose money at some point. There is no investor on earth who has avoided taking a loss. It is simply impossible to do so. No one has a success rate of 100%. Even individuals like Warren Buffett or George Soros have experienced *MANY* losses in their careers.

Position sizing is how successful traders weather these inevitable losses without blowing up their accounts. Provided you never blow up your account, over time you will begin to make money (and in the long run, potentially a LOT of money). This brings us to a critical difference I've noticed between how novice investors and more sophisticated investors think about their investments.

How Inexperienced Investors Think About an Investment

Inexperienced or novice investors usually approach a trade from the perspective of *"how much money can I make?"* or even worse, from some vague notion of "profit" that they haven't even quantified in terms of a specific dollar amount. This kind of thinking is extremely dangerous for several reasons.

1. Investing, while an art form, requires **precision**.

2. Emotional thinking, or even worse, hope, clouds your judgement. As soon as your judgement is clouded, you are in danger of losing a LOT of money in the markets.

Regarding #1, I've met plenty of novice investors who open positions based on "guesses" or by "ball-parking" an investment. Typically doing this has resulted in them losing a LOT of money. Moreover, I've yet to meet any successful investor who does this. This is not to say that intuition or "gut feeling" doesn't play some part in investing. Successful investors typically have a solid intuition concerning their trades. But they **_always_ integrate risk management into their trading**.

As for #2 (emotional thinking clouds a trader's judgement), I personally know several successful money managers who will completely step back from the markets if their personal lives are chaotic or in a crisis. If they are forced to remain active in the markets due to fund requirements, they reduce position sizes to the point that being wrong will result in relatively small losses. And if they have total discretion over their funds, most of them will simply **stop opening new positions altogether and shift largely to cash.**

Why do this?

These people know that during a time of personal turmoil, their judgement is clouded. As a result of this, they don't risk capital during those times. Instead, they monitor the markets and focus on getting their head straight before they start risking capital again.

Again, **successful investors _always_ integrate risk management in their investing.** This includes the risk of emotions clouding one's judgement. And as a result of this, these individuals approach a trade from a completely different perspective than inexperienced traders.

How Successful Investors Think About an Investment

Successful or experienced traders always approach a trade from the perspective of _"how much money can I potentially lose on this position?"_ They do this because they know that every investment involves risk. Even U.S. Treasuries, which are considered to be "risk free" in the sense that the government can always print money to pay you back, can lose money by falling in price. And no matter how talented you become at reading the markets, there is always the chance that you are dead wrong on a particular investment.

Thus, successful investors always consider that they might be totally wrong on a potential investment and then work to assess how large of a position to take based on the volatility and other details of the investment. Doing this means that their focus is always on risk management as opposed to greed or fear or some other emotion that might cloud their judgement. And that is how they last and profit as investors.

Remember, if you can routinely profit from the markets, even if those profits are relatively small amounts at first, over time your portfolio will grow. Sure, it might not be in a week or two, but several years down the line, provided you maintain your discipline, you'll be sitting on a good size portfolio. At that point, locking in the profits from high probability/low risk trades will mean **making thousands, if not tens of thousands of dollars**, even on a relatively small percentage gain of just 5%.

This is why successful or experienced traders approach each investment from a perspective of "risk management," not greed or some other emotion. Doing this reduces the odds of them suffering a catastrophic loss. These individuals know that provided they do this, over time they will amass riches.

Now that we've established the difference between how successful and inexperienced traders think about a given trade, let's consider how to determine the appropriate position size for a hypothetical trade.

How To Size a Position

Personally, I've found the best way to discern the appropriate position size for a given investment is to start with the largest loss of capital I'm willing to stomach, and work backwards. Personally, I use a total portfolio loss of 1%, but for some investors it might be less or more depending on their risk appetites.

Let's say your total portfolio is $100,000. Based on my personal risk management protocol (avoiding a total portfolio loss greater than 1% in any given position), this would mean that the most you are willing to lose on any given position is $1,000.

Now, not all investments are the same. Some are more speculative than others. So, let's apply this risk management framework to a hypothetical speculative position and a hypothetical core position.

Let's use Shopify (NASDAQ: SHOP) as the speculative position.

SHOP is an ecommerce platform that would be considered a "growth stock." What I mean by this is that SHOP has spent much of its time as a publicly traded company without producing a profit. Moreover, the company doesn't pay a dividend. Thus, the primary appeal of the company's business is that its revenue stream is growing rapidly.

So why even consider owning SHOP?

Because SHOP shares are EXTREMELY volatile. And this volatility can result in significant returns when SHOP shares rally. It is not unusual for SHOP shares to move 5% or even 20% in a single week. And during the bubble from 2019 to 2021, SHOP shares rose over 1,700%. So, you need to build this volatility into your trading model to establish your position size. Since SHOP is a speculative position (an investor is likely buying shares for a trade, NOT as a long-term investment) we are using weeks rather than months for our risk parameters here.

Obviously, there is no guarantee that buying SHOP shares will make you money. But by using this kind of risk management, you GREATLY reduce the odds of losing more than 1% of your portfolio on this position.

Now let's consider the risk management for a non-speculative, or core position. Let's use one of Warren Buffett's favorite investments: the Coca-Cola Company (NYSE: KO).

KO has been in business for over a century. Coca-Cola or Coke is one of the most recognized products on the planet. The company is also one of the most profitable businesses with a history of focusing on shareholder returns: e.g., KO has raised its dividends for 60 years. Put simply, KO is a completely different business from SHOP. When you buy KO, you're buying a business that has proven to be a cash-flow generating behemoth for *decades*.

Because of this profitability, the stability of KO's business, and the company's size, KO shares tend to be less volatile: it's highly unusual for the company to move more than **10% in a month**. Note I'm using months, not weeks for my risk management framework here because KO is not a speculative investment: an investor would likely be buying KO for the long term (months, if not years) rather than as a speculative trade.

Consider that between 2000 and 2023, the stock market experienced multiple multi-year bear markets. Indeed, between 2000 and 2013, the S&P 500 effectively traded sideways. And yet, despite this poor performance by stocks for much of the last 24 years, an investor who bought KO's stock in early 2000 would have generated astonishing returns. The cost to acquire 100 shares of KO stock on January 3, 2000, was ~$4,800. Today, those same shares would be worth ~$49,000. And that's NOT based on reinvesting dividends!

Again, KO is what you would consider a "Core" position for your portfolio. It's the kind of company you want to buy and hold for the long term (months, if not years). And if KO shares collapse due to a crash or some other rare event, you'd want to buy MORE of them rather than panic selling.

Again, this analysis *doesn't* mean you won't lose money on KO stock; it simply ensures that it is unlikely you will lose more than 1% of your total portfolio doing so. This brings us to the final and perhaps trickiest component of my risk management framework for active stock investors: having an exit strategy or plan for when things work out, or don't.

How and When to Sell a Stock

Warren Buffett once stated that his preferred holding period is "forever." Unless you intend to model your strategy after him, at some point you will need to sell the stocks you buy.

There are two instances of selling we need to focus on:

1. Closing out losses.

2. Locking in profits.

I realize the above information sounds obvious at first glance. After all, in investing NOTHING is set in stone until you hit "sell" on a given trade. However, it's one thing to say, *"I know when to sell this trade"* and something else entirely to be sitting on a large profit or a loss and having to hit "sell."

Let's start with the losses first.

How to Close Out a Loss

As I keep emphasizing, the single most important thing for an active trader to focus on is **avoiding a catastrophic loss**. For this reason, I suggest using a Stop Loss on whatever percentage loss results in your position hitting the maximum loss of capital permitted by your risk management.

If you're unfamiliar with the concept of a "Stop Loss" it's simply a rule stating that you would sell a position the moment it hits a certain dollar loss, thereby "stopping" the "loss" from growing larger. So, if your portfolio is $100,000 in size, and the maximum allowable loss of capital on this portfolio is 1% ($1,000), **then you would sell any position the moment your dollar loss hits that amount.**

This should be a HARD rule, meaning you don't deviate from it under any circumstances. Stop Losses are meant to override one's emotional thinking while sitting on a losing position, e.g., *"it will come back," "I should average in to get a better original buy price,"* etc.

However, there will be many times in which an investment is a bad one, but it doesn't necessarily hit your stop loss. After all, why wait for a bad trade to hit the MAXIMUM allowable loss of capital before hitting "sell"? Wouldn't it be better to get out of a bad trade sooner rather than later? And how do you know when to do this?

To answer that, we need to refer to Rule #1 from our framework: we only make high probability/low risk investments. So, you should sell when a trade goes from being a high probability/low risk trade to a low probability/high risk trade.

Let me explain…

In investing, many times you will end up being "early," meaning that the price move you anticipate doesn't happen for some time. In terms of deciding whether to sell the stock or not, I find the critical criteria is determining whether the investment is simply moving sideways while you wait, or if it is going *against* you. Let me give you an example.

Let's say that you were bullish on Exxon Mobil (NYSE: XOM) in early 2023. At that time, the company was trading at a valuation well below its five-year averages for its Price to Earnings (P/E) and Price to Cash Flow (P/CF) multiples. On top of this, XOM shares were moving in a strong uptrend (see chart below).

An active investor would note that XOM shares had dipped down to test their long-term trendline (gray line in the chart below) and use this opportunity to buy, assuming that XOM shares would "bounce" off this line and begin another leg up just as they did in late December 2021 and late September 2022.

Chart 19: Exxon Mobil Corp Share Price (2021-2023)

Note: Chart courtesy of StockCharts.com

Now, let's assume that you are early and XOM shares DO NOT begin to rally immediately; instead, they begin to chop sideways. Do you sell and move on to the next trade? Based on our risk management protocol, the answer is "no." Your thesis has yet to be proven incorrect. XOM shares remain at their trendline, and the likelihood of a rally remains a high probability/low risk setup.

Now, let's say that instead of chopping sideways, XOM shares collapse by

5% and break through their trendline. In this scenario, XOM shares have broken their uptrend. Momentum has turned downwards. And XOM shares are now well below the price at which you bought. So, you would need a significant rally just to break even.

In this scenario, your trade has now gone from being a high probability/low risk trade to a low probability/high risk trade (the odds of a significant rally are now much lower). So, while your total loss of capital might be well below the maximum allowable amount, **it's a good idea to sell XOM and move on.** After all, your thesis (XOM is in an uptrend and will begin its next leg up) has proven incorrect. And the odds of things working out in your favor are now low, so why wait to lose more money?

So again, when it comes to selling a loss, some basic guidelines to use are:

1. Is the investment moving sideways, or is it moving against you?

2. If it's moving against you, has your thesis been disproven?

If the answer to #2 is "yes," I suggest closing out the trade even if the loss is much smaller than your Stop Loss.

Now let's talk about when to lock in a profit.

When to Lock in a Profit

Profit-taking is one of the most difficult aspects of investing. However, my overall view on this subject is best explained by the following two quotes:

"I made a fortune selling too early."
— J.P. Morgan

"I never invest at the bottom, and I always sell too soon."
— Nathan Rothschild

Let's be clear here: making money from investing is difficult. So, when a trade has generated a decent profit, I typically prefer to sell. Remember, I am approaching this situation from the perspective of a short-term trader, not a long-term investor.

"But wait a minute, Graham," you're no doubt thinking, *"if you sell now, you miss out on larger profits."*

There is some truth to this. But if you have properly identified who you are as an investor, and you're primarily making low risk/high probability investments, you should have a decent idea of what is likely to happen for a given investment.

Consider our example of Exxon Mobil (XOM) from a few pages ago. If I were investing in this company in early 2023, I would likely be buying with the expectation of selling once shares get near $110. That'd be a nice 10% gain. After all, based on the price action of XOM shares, a 10% gain in a couple of weeks' time is a reasonable expectation. During bull runs, XOM shares have done this numerous times. Moreover, the reason I'd sell at $110 as opposed to holding in anticipation of a larger return is that XOM has a cluster of weekly closes at $110. This cluster would be considered "resistance" meaning that XOM shares would have a difficult time breaking above this level easily.

Am I potentially missing out on a larger return? Well, XOM shares had previously gone up from $60 to $100 per share from January 2022 to June 2022. That's a massive 66% return. By settling for a 10% return in two weeks, I might look foolish. But there's no reason I wouldn't trade XOM numerous times during a given six-month period. And I'd prefer to lock in a high probability/low risk 10% return multiple times, rather than banking on a low probability 66% return once.

Again, this is what works for me. I know who I am as a trader. I know my personality and my risk profile. Yours might be different than mine. But if you are just starting out as an active investor, I would urge you to lock in profits when you can.

Why?

Because you're building your confidence and knowledge. You're not trying to get rich quickly, you're trying to develop your skills as an investor. Seeing your account balance grow, even if it's by a little at a time, is highly beneficial from a psychological perspective.

Simply put, in investing, no one goes broke by locking in a profit. Do it enough times for a long enough time period and you will get rich. And that's the reason you started actively investing in stocks in the first place, isn't it?

We've covered a lot of material in this chapter, so let's run a brief review before ending it.

1. Successful investing starts with figuring out your investor profile. There are no wrong answers to this. You're simply trying to figure out who you are in terms of risk appetite or your approach to the markets. Once you figure out who you are as an investor, FOCUS on strategies that use your strengths and downplay your weaknesses. Do NOT deviate from these.

2. Investing in stocks ALWAYS involves a significant level of risk. Because this risk never goes away, no matter how skilled you become as an investor, the single most important skill for an investor to develop is the ability to avoid catastrophic losses.

3. One means of avoiding a catastrophic loss is to do significant research before making your investment decision. While this

doesn't mean you'll always be right, it does reduce the odds of you being completely wrong and suffering a catastrophic loss. Some examples of research that can move the odds in your favor when it comes to investing:

    a. Detailed and extensive knowledge of the company's underlying business.

    b. Detailed and extensive knowledge concerning the stock's price action.

    c. Some kind of specialized knowledge concerning the company's products, IP, etc. We all are experts on something, chances are there are publicly traded companies whose businesses are in your area of expertise.

4. Focus on high probability/low risk investments.

    a. Hollywood and the media like to focus on "long shot" ideas as the source of riches, but in reality, the odds of these working in your favor are less than that of being struck by lightning.

    b. By focusing on high probability/low risk investments, over time you will grow your portfolio to the point that even a small gain will mean significant dollar returns.

5. Carefully size your position.

    a. Start with the maximum amount of capital you're willing to lose on a single position and work your way backwards.

    b. Build the volatility of the company's price action as well as the nature of the trade (speculative vs. core) into your framework.

6. Have an exit strategy or plan for when things work out, or don't.

    a. Use a Stop Loss to insure a loss never exceeds the maximum amount of capital you're willing to lose on a single position.

    b. If you're early on an investment, determine whether the trade is moving sideways while you wait, or if it's going against you.

c. If the trade is going against you, sell it as soon as it becomes a high risk/low probability trade, even if it has yet to hit your Stop Loss.

The above framework is by no means exhaustive. However, if you follow the principles I've laid out here, you'll avoid most of the major mistakes that individual investors typically make. Provided you do that, over time you *will* make money from your investments. And if you maintain your discipline and risk management, eventually you will make a LOT of money. But always remember, investing is like plumbing, dentistry, or the law: it takes years of work to get to the point at which you make serious money from it.

Conclusion

Writing this book was something of an impossible undertaking. For one thing, the financial world has changed dramatically in the last few years. Things that were previously deemed impossible (shutting down the economy, the Fed printing $5 trillion in six months) have happened. And I have little doubt that things that sound impossible today, such as the future monetary policies I laid out in Chapter 4, will eventually unfold as well.

Moreover, the economy and financial system are far more difficult to navigate today than they were for most of 1982-2022 and especially from 2008 through 2022. During that period, there was a secular bull market in bonds that meant yields gradually dropped over time as debt became cheaper and cheaper to service. That time period is over.

Regardless of whether or not Treasury yields drop during the next recession or crisis, we are no longer in a secular bull market for bonds. Investing will be far more complicated and involve greater risks. But as I've tried to emphasize throughout this book, market risks translate to larger potential gains as well as larger potential losses.

This is why I emphasize risk management in the second portion of this book. Going forward it's going to be critical that you think in terms of risk management, particularly since any investment strategy that was predicated on the decline of bond yields is now outdated (again the era of low yields is over).

Life after the bubble is strange, but it is also exciting. If you are unwilling to adapt, you will find it challenging. But if you are excited by change and see opportunity in new challenges, then you should do very well indeed.

In the abyss, we can either be frightened or we can find out who we really are. And since self-knowledge is perhaps the single most valuable skill an investor can have, I'd urge you to opt for the latter. After all, if anything has become clear in the last five years, it's that policymakers are willing to implement things that were previously unthinkable. Knowing who you are is essential in that kind of environment.

For those of you seeking additional assistance and insights, I publish several trading products through my publishing company Summers Capital Press (https://summerscapitalpress.com/).

I also provide consulting services for individual investors as well as institutions through my other company, Summers Capital Consulting (https://summerscapitalconsulting.com/).

Endnotes

1   U.S. Bureau of Economic Analysis, Gross Domestic Product [GDP], retrieved from FRED, Federal Reserve Bank of St. Louis; https://fred.stlouisfed.org/series/GDP, March 4, 2024.

   Board of Governors of the Federal Reserve System (US), All Sectors; Debt Securities and Loans; Liability, Level (DISCONTINUED) [TCMDO], retrieved from FRED, Federal Reserve Bank of St. Louis; https://fred.stlouisfed.org/series/TCMDO, March 4, 2024.

2   Board of Governors of the Federal Reserve System (US), All Federal Reserve Banks: Total Assets [WALCL], retrieved from FRED, Federal Reserve Bank of St. Louis; https://fred.stlouisfed.org/series/WALCL, March 4, 2024.

3   JP. Cabinet Office, Gross Domestic Product for Japan [JPNNGDP], retrieved from FRED, Federal Reserve Bank of St. Louis; https://fred.stlouisfed.org/series/JPNNGDP, March 4, 2024.

4   "Japan 10-Year Bond Yield Historical Data." *Investing.com*,

   https://www.investing.com/rates-bonds/japan-10-year-bond-yield-historical-data

5   United States 10-Year Bond Yield Historical Data." *Investing.com*,

   https://www.investing.com/rates-bonds/u.s.-10-year-bond-yield-historical-data

6   U.S. Bureau of Labor Statistics, Consumer Price Index for All Urban Consumers: All Items in U.S. City Average [CPIAUCSL], retrieved from FRED, Federal Reserve Bank of St. Louis; https://fred.stlouisfed.org/series/CPIAUCSL, March 4, 2024.

7   United States 2-Year Bond Yield Historical Data." *Investing.com*, https://www.investing.com/rates-bonds/u.s.-2-year-bond-yield-historical-data

8   Board of Governors of the Federal Reserve System (US), Federal Funds Effective Rate [FEDFUNDS], retrieved from FRED, Federal Reserve Bank of St. Louis; https://fred.stlouisfed.org/series/FEDFUNDS, March 4, 2024.

9   U.S. Census Bureau and U.S. Department of Housing and Urban Development, Median Sales Price of Houses Sold for the United States [MSPUS], retrieved from FRED, Federal Reserve Bank of St. Louis; https://fred.stlouisfed.org/series/MSPUS, February 29, 2024.